Connie von Hundertmark

Cruise Ship Cookbook

Cover design and illustrations by Barry Moyer.

Garlic Press

A Garlic Press Edition
© Copyright National Press, Inc. 1986
7508 Wisconsin Avenue
Bethesda, Maryland 20814
(800) NA-BOOKS

Library of Congress Cataloging-in-Publication Data

Von Hundertmark, Connie, 1946-
  Cruise ship cookbook.

  "A Garlic Press book."
  Includes index.
  1. Cookery. 2. Cruise ships. I. Title.
TX652.V65 1986   641.5'753   86-12843
ISBN 0-915765-33-0

for Gretchen

Acknowledgements

Many cruise ship companies and individuals have contributed greatly to the compilation of this book, including Windjammer Barefoot Cruises, Norwegian Caribbean Lines, Hellenic Mediterranean Lines, Sun Line Cruises, Presidential Nile Cruises, Home Lines, Premier Cruise Lines, Continental Waterways, Floating through Europe, Holland America Line, Highland Steamboat Holidays, Royal Cruise Line, Society Expeditions Cruises, American Hawaii Cruises, Delta Queen Steamboat Company, Sea Breeze Florida Keys Cruises, Out O'Mystic Schooner Cruises, Exploration Holidays and Cruises, Mid-Lakes Navigation Company, Susan Klein and C. Douglas House.

Table of Contents

Introduction	7
Part I: Caribbean Cuisine	9
Chapter One: Windjammer	10
Chapter Two: Norwegian Caribbean Lines	15
Part II: Mediterranean Cooking	19
Chapter Three: The Hellenic Mediterranean Lines	20
Chapter Four: Sun Line Cruises	25
Chapter Five: Presidential Nile Cruises	35
Chapter Six: Home Lines	43
Part III: A Taste of Europe	57
Chapter Seven: Premier Cruise Lines	58
Chapter Eight: Continental Waterways	74
Chapter Nine: Floating through Europe	80
Chapter Ten: Holland America Line	98
Chapter Eleven: Highland Steamboat Holidays	102
Part IV: Recipes from Around the World	109
Chapter Twelve: Royal Cruise Line	110
Chapter Thirteen: Society Expeditions Cruises	122
Part V: American Dishes	127
Chapter Fourteen: American Hawaii Cruises	128
Chapter Fifteen: Delta Queen Steamboat Company	131
Chapter Sixteen: Sea Breeze Florida Keys Cruises	141
Chapter Seventeen: Out O'Mystic Schooner Cruises	144
Chapter Eighteen: Exploration Holidays and Cruises	148
Chapter Nineteen: Mid-Lakes Navigation Company	161
Index	167

Introduction

Whether you're gliding through the brilliant blue waters of the Caribbean, sailing past the midwestern fall foliage along the Ohio River or basking on a ship's deck in the dazzling, Hawaiian sun, the highlight of any major cruise ship is the sumptuous food.

Wherever the port-of-call—St. Thomas, New Orleans, Acapulco, Honolulu, Anchorage or Istanbul—all the major cruise lines pride themselves on their bountiful and excellent cuisine. It is a rare passenger indeed who does not allow himself the sybaritic indulgence of partaking in all of the dining pleasure his cruise ship provides—breakfast, lunch, afternoon tea, cocktail hour, dinner and the midnight groaning board buffet.

Vacationing on a cruise ship is the time to cast away all morbid thoughts of dieting and weight loss. Worry about that when you return to reality. For now, for your voyage—it's bon appétit!

The master chefs of many major cruise ships have graciously shared some of their gourmet recipes. Some of the foods are ethnic, some traditionally served at the captain's formal dinner, some the most often requested by passengers and some just the chef's particular specialty or favorite.

Now you can recreate the shipboard dining experience in your own kitchen—then sit back, relax and pretend you hear the waves lapping, feel the sea wind blowing and haven't a care in the world!

—Connie von Hundertmark

Part One
Caribbean Cuisine

Chapter One

Windjammer

Picture yourself on a four masted, tall sailing ship, lazing through the Caribbean, sipping rum sizzles. Imagine a cruise on a schooner that only stops at romantic, deserted islands. Conjure up an image of yourself helping to hoist the sails of a ship right from yesteryear in all its grandeur while you head out for the British Virgin Islands, West Indies, Bahamas or Grenadine Islands. All this can come true on the Windjammer Barefoot Cruises, a millionaire's holiday for everyone to enjoy aboard the great sailing ships that have almost vanished from the seas.

There are seven tall ships in the Windjammer fleet, each breathtakingly beautiful. The ships served varied purposes in the past—as training vessels for the French Navy, as floating palaces for English royalty. Aristotle Onassis presented one ship—the Fantome, the largest four masted schooner in the world—to Grace Kelly and Prince Rainier as a wedding present. Another was the private yacht of the Vanderbilts. The Mandalay, a luxury sailing ship, was the leisure ship of E.F. Hutton, founder of the stock brokerage firm.

Windjammer

These voyages last from three days to ten months. You can island hop or sail around the world. Windjammer cruises are very casual. The only time you wear shoes is when you leave the ship for island exploration. The rest of the time, it's leisurely, laid-back fun on board.

A complimentary Bloody Mary is served with breakfast, potent 140 double proof rum punch is generously poured at cocktail time, and the wine is free with dinner. You'll find that the ships' captains often use any excuse at all to uncork the champagne—to celebrate toga contests, reward the most passengers to fit in a shower stall, or honor the party brave enough to toss the captain overboard during some shipboard hijinks.

Buffet luncheon on Windjammer Barefoot Cruises.

Cruise Ship Cookbook

These voyages are paradisiacal party cruises with lots of rum and lots of good Caribbean food. Chef Ralph Chedda of the Bahamas Yankee Trader likes to whip up the following dishes. For barbecues, family reunions or any other large gathering, these recipes for crowds will be sure-fire pleasers:

Caribbean Dark Bread

9 cups white flour
10 cups rye or pumpernickel flour
¾ cup cocoa
⅓ cup yeast
3 tablespoons caraway seed
6 cups water
1 cup molasses
6 tablespoons margarine
3 tablespoons sugar
3 tablespoons salt

In mixer bowl, combine white flour, cocoa, yeast and caraway seed. In saucepan, heat water, molasses, margarine, sugar and salt until lukewarm, stirring occasionally to melt margarine. Add contents to flour mixture. Beat at low speed for 1 minute, then at high speed for 3 minutes. Stir in rye or pumpernickel flour to make a soft but not sticky dough. Cover bowl and let sit for 30 minutes. Punch down and shape into 6 loaves and place on 2 greased baking sheets. Brush with oil and slash top. Let rise for 60 minutes. Bake at 400° for 25 to 30 minutes. Makes 6 loaves. Loaves may be frozen.

Windjammer

Gingersnap Cookies

2½ cups shortening
3 cups sugar
3 eggs
¾ cup molasses
6 cups flour
1 tablespoon ground ginger
2 tablespoons cinnamon
1½ teaspoons salt

Cream shortening and sugar. Beat in eggs and add molasses. Add remaining ingredients and mix well. Form into small balls and roll in sugar. Bake at 350° for 15 minutes. Makes 5 dozen.

Windjammer Caesar Salad

1 raw egg
1 clove garlic, finely chopped
1 teaspoon lime juice
1 tablespoon dry mustard
2 tablespoons Parmesan cheese, grated
1 tablespoon soy sauce
1 tablespoon white vinegar
¼ cup anchovies
2½ tablespoons olive oil
3 heads romaine lettuce
2 cup prepared croutons

Mix together all ingredients except lettuce and croutons. Tear lettuce into bite-sized pieces. Pour dressing over lettuce and croutons and serve at once. Serves 10.

Island Noodles Alfredo

1 pound egg noodles
¾ cup olive oil
1 large onion, minced
1 clove garlic, minced
½ cup margarine
1 cup Parmesan cheese, grated
½ cup dried parsley flakes or fresh parsley
2 small cans evaporated milk

Cook noodles until just tender. Rinse with cold water. Cook onion in olive oil until tender. Add garlic and cook for 2 minutes. Add margarine and melt but don't cook. Add mixture to noodles. Sprinkle with Parmesan cheese and parsley. When ready to serve, pour scalded evaporated milk over all. Serves 20.

Chapter Two

Norwegian Caribbean Lines

Casinos, cabaret reviews, outdoor barbecues, shipboard Olympics, astrology lessons, masquerade parties, fitness classes, grandparents' parties, singles-only extravaganzas are just a small part of the lavish and plentiful activities aboard the five ships on the Norwegian Caribbean Lines. From Miami to Mexico, St. Thomas to San Juan, Jamaica to Nassau, the Grand Cayman Island to the cruise line's very own private Caribbean Island, you are certain to see the M.S. Southward, M.S. Starward, M.S. Skyward, M.S. Sunward II or the S.S. Norway parting the water.

The atmosphere can be as relaxing as you want it or a nonstop party—whatever is your liking aboard any of these ocean liners.

The S.S. Norway is the largest ship in the world, with 65,000 feet of open deck, a dozen bars, lounges and nightclubs, and three pools. It carries 1,864 passengers and has a crew of 800. Since its maiden voyage in June of 1980, each cruise on the Norway has featured entertainment from a major recording or film star. And the food aboard this stellar line is as topnotch as the entertainment. Here are two particular favorites of Executive Chef Max Putier:

Paillard of Salmon with Sorrel Sauce

3 pounds fresh salmon, cut in very thin scallops
½ cup oil
2 scant teaspoons (coffeespoons) sorrel (found in gourmet shops)
1 cup dry vermouth
1 cup white wine
3 scant teaspoons (coffeespoons) shallots, very finely chopped
1 cup cream
Salt and pepper to taste

To prepare sauce: In saucepan, reduce white wine, Vermouth and shallots to 1 cup. Add cream and reduce again to thicken. Season and add sorrel.

To prepare salmon: Salt and pepper salmon scallops and place in frying pan with hot oil. Cook for a few seconds on each side. Do not let them dry out. Serve salmon on warm plates covered with sorrel sauce. Serves 6.

Norwegian Caribbean Lines

Chicken Calvados

4 boneless chicken breasts
2 apples, sliced
1 jigger apple brandy
½ cup white wine
½ cup heavy cream
½ cup flour
Salt and pepper to taste

Roll chicken breasts in flour. Dust off excess amount and sauté in hot oil until golden brown. Add apple slices and cook for a few seconds. Flambé with apple brandy, add white wine, let reduce and add heavy cream. Cook until done, about 20 minutes, and season with salt and pepper. Serves 4.

Enjoy luscious dining aboard the Norwegian Caribbean Lines.

Part Two
Mediterranean Cooking

Chapter Three

The Hellenic Mediterranean Lines

A seven day Greek Island cruise through the fabled Aegean might be just what the doctor ordered to make you forget all your worries. There is a crew member for every two passengers on board the Hellenic Mediterranean Lines' splendid ship Aquarius, and service is unusually personal for a large ocean liner. This beautiful ship has all the intimate style and elegant decor of a private yacht and every amenity of the larger ocean liners.

Everyday offers a new itinerary to a different Greek Island. You can follow the passage of time of the ancient civilizations of the Phoenicians, Dorians, Romans and Byzantines:

First, you'll visit Santorini. A volcanic island that nearly disappeared in 1450 B.C., it may be the source of legends of the lost city of Atlantis. There you can take a donkey ride up a 700 foot cliff to view the splendor of the entire island.

Then, travel to Crete to the ruins of the palace of Minos. The oldest palace excavated in Europe, it was built in 1800 B.C.

Hellenic Mediterranean Lines

After that, it's on to Rhodes, where you'll visit the castle of the Knights of St. John, the Palace of the Grand Masters, and the Acropolis at Lindos.

But the trip's not over yet! On Kusadasi, you'll see the ruins of Epheses where the Apostles St. John and St. Paul preached. Other ancient visitors included Androcles, Pythagoras, Alexander the Great, Marc Antony, Cleopatra and the Virgin Mary.

In Istanbul, you'll admire the lavish structures built by Byzantine Emperors and Ottoman Sultans, and, time and weather permitting, you'll tour Mykonos, a popular residence for artists and intellectuals.

Return from your trip back in time to the realities of today by hoisting a cold glass of kir or a scotch on the rocks at the ship's cocktail bar—and don't forget to sample the ouzo to get into the real Grecian spirit.

The tables in the dining room of the Aquarius are exquisitely appointed with Rosenthal china, fine crystal and Christofle silverware—the perfect setting for delicious Greek cuisine. The traditions may be ancient, but all the food is the original creation of the master chef and his staff.

Avgolemono Chicken Soup

1 small to medium chicken
½ pound rice
3 to 5 eggs, newly laid
Lemon juice
Salt and pepper to taste

In soup kettle, boil chicken and rice very slowly until chicken is practically falling off the bone. In large bowl, beat eggs and lemon juice. While beating, gradually add small quantities of hot chicken broth until contents of bowl are doubled and are very hot. Now pour contents of bowl into soup kettle and salt and pepper to taste. Black pepper brings out the flavor of the soup, so be sure to have a pepper mill on the table. For a change, you may also serve it with a little powdered cinnamon sprinkled on top.

Loukoumades
(A Greek dessert)

4 ounces yeast
2 cups milk
1 cup water, plus additional
1 teaspoon salt
4 cups flour
Sugar, for garnish
Honey, for garnish
Cinnamon, for garnish

In basin, dissolve yeast in lukewarm milk and water. Add salt and a little flour to make dough. Allow to rise in warm place. Add rest of flour and enough lukewarm water to make batter soft enough to drop from spoon. Cover basin and allow to stand 5 to 6 hours until batter starts to bubble on top. Batter is then ready for frying. In deep skillet, heat 3 to 4 inches of oil until steaming. Drop batter from spoon and fry until golden brown. Dip spoon in cup of cold water each time to prevent batter from sticking. When Loukoumades are fried, drain them on absorbent paper. Arrange on platter and sprinkle with sugar, honey and cinnamon. Serve hot. Makes 2 dozen.

Giovetsi
(Roast Lamb with Pasta Giovetsi Style)

Leg or shoulder of lamb
1 to 2 cloves garlic
Salt and pepper to taste
1 onion, sliced
6 ounce can tomato paste
4 to 6 cups boiling water
1 pound pasta, rice or macaroni
Parmesan cheese and/or feta or casseri cheese

Prepare lamb and season to taste. With sharp knife, make slits in meat. Insert garlic in slits and sprinkle with salt and pepper. Place meat in baking pan, add onion slices, and bake at 425° for 30 minutes. Baste meat with lemon juice and return to oven until meat is done and well browned. Remove meat and onions from baking pan and keep warm. Add tomato paste and boiling water to pan drippings. Use 4 cups water for rice, 6 or more for pasta. Slowly sprinkle rice or pasta in baking pan and replace it in oven. Stir occasionally. When rice or pasta is cooked, remove from oven and allow to stand covered with a towel for a few minutes. Arrange on platter with meat, onions and cheese. Serves 8.

Skordalia
(Bread Salad)

This dish is especially good when served with fish. The chefs of the Hellenic Mediterranean Lines serve it with the salted, fried codfish of Iceland.

4 to 8 slices white bread, crusts trimmed
10 cloves garlic, crushed
1 cup olive oil
Salt to taste

Moisten bread and squeeze out excess water. Add crushed garlic and beat mixture while adding salt and oil, a spoonful at a time. Beat until creamy. Serves 6 to 8.

Chapter Four

Sun Line Cruises

Designed as luxurious floating homes, the three ships in the Sun Line "Stellas" fleet offer the ultimate in opulent Greek hospitality. The all-Greek staff is very friendly, and your waiter and bartender will soon know your name and your favorite drinks.

Cruising the Eastern Mediterranean from Greece to Turkey to Egypt to Israel—as well as the Amazon River, Panama Canal, Rio de Janeiro and Caribbean—the Stella Solaris, Stella Maris and Stella Oceanis take you to exotic sites you've seen only in the pages of *National Geographic*. You can walk barefoot through island villages or along white beaches, explore ancient ruins or tropical jungles, and visit famous sites like the Rock of Gibraltar or the coast where Columbus first landed. You will see man-made wonders, such as the Panama Canal, and natural wonders, such as Angel Falls, the tallest cascade in the world, fifteen times higher than the Niagara. Or you can celebrate at the spectacular Carnival in Rio, an event that seems to become more colorful and extravagant every year.

Cruise Ship Cookbook

Wherever they travel, the Sun Line ships feature Greek and American cuisine. Their ports are gemlike and their itineraries are to be envied, but the fun on these cruises —besides the belly dancing, bouzouki players, and Las Vegas nightclub entertainment—is chow time. From appetizers to sinfully rich desserts, Greek specialties are the order of the day. Master Chef Athanassios Livadas can help you duplicate the Stellas dining experience in your own kitchen.

Cocktail Meatballs

1 pound ground beef
½ pound ground lamb
3 tablespoons olive oil
1 onion, grated
1 clove garlic, minced
2 eggs
4 tablespoons parsley, finely chopped
½ teaspoon oregano
½ teaspoon sweet basil
10 slices bread, soaked in water and squeezed dry
2 tablespoons ouzo
½ cup white wine

Coat a large baking dish with olive oil. Combine remaining ingredients, excepting ¼ cup wine. Knead well, form bite-sized balls, and put in baking dish. Bake in hot oven at 475° for about 20 to 30 minutes. Pour remaining wine over baking dish, and turn meatballs. Bake an additional 10 minutes. Keep warm in chafing dish until serving. Serves 6 or more.

Fried Zucchini

1 pound zucchini
½ cup soy sauce
Salt to taste
1 cup flour

Wash zucchini, slice very thin, and sprinkle with soy sauce and salt. Let stand 10 to 15 minutes. Dip in flour and fry in hot oil until crisp and golden. Serves 6 or more.

Tzatziki
(Cucumber Salad)

2 cucumbers
¼ cup vinegar
1 pound yogurt, or ½ yogurt and ½ sour cream
4 cloves garlic, crushed
½ cup olive oil
2 teaspoons dill
Salt and pepper to taste

Peel cucumbers and grate coarsely. Add salt and vinegar, mix well, and put in strainer to drain for 30 minutes. Gently mix yogurt with garlic, oil and dill. Add cucumbers and pepper and toss lightly. Serve as dip with crackers or with thinly sliced, fried zucchini (see previous recipe). Serves 6.

Taramosalata
(Caviar)

For something different, you can use two medium boiled potatoes in place of the bread.

    7 ounce jar Tarama or other caviar
    7 slices white bread
    4 tablespoons onion, grated
    1 cup olive oil
    2 lemons, squeezed for juice
    Parsley, chopped (optional)
    Black Greek olives, thinly sliced (optional)

Trim crust from bread, soak in water and squeeze dry. Put caviar in blender at low speed until creamy. Blend in onion and bread. Slowly add oil and lemon juice, alternating until mixture is white and creamy. Garnish with parsley and/or olives. Can be served as dip or as hôrs d'oeuvres with crackers.

The Stella Solaris.

Sun Line Cruises

Eggplant Salad

2 large eggplants
1 medium onion
3 tablespoons parsley
2 cloves garlic
2 fresh salad tomatoes
1 tablespoon mayonnaise
¼ cup lemon juice
¼ cup olive oil
Salt and pepper to taste

Pierce eggplants with fork and bake at 350° for 1 hour until soft. Cool and peel. Finely chop onion and parsley and crush garlic. Coarsely chop eggplants and tomatoes. In a bowl, toss lightly all ingredients including oil, lemon juice, and mayonnaise. Serve at room temperature or chilled. Serves 6.

Egg–Cheese Puffs

5 eggs
½ cup flour
1½ teaspoons baking powder
1 teaspoon salt
1½ cups cubed Kefalotiri or a hard cheese
Butter or shortening

Beat eggs well. Sift flour with baking powder and salt and add to eggs. Add cheese. Mix well. Brown butter or shortening in frying pan and drop in spoonfuls of batter to fry. Turn puffs with slotted spoon carefully to avoid piercing. Drain on paper towels. Serve hot. Serves 6.

Moussaka with Eggplant

1 pound chopped beef
½ cup onions, finely chopped
1½ medium tomatoes, peeled and sliced
Parsley
4 ounces tomato paste
Salt and pepper to taste
1 large eggplant, peeled and sliced
2 medium potatoes, peeled and sliced
½ cup butter
½ cup flour
2 cups milk, scalded
1 dash nutmeg
2 eggs, slightly beaten
½ cup Parmesan cheese

In skillet, brown chopped beef. Drain. Sauté onions until soft but not brown. Add tomatoes, parsley and tomato paste and cook for about 10 to 15 minutes. Add salt and pepper and set aside. In frying pan, quickly fry eggplant in hot oil until golden, adding a little oil at a time because eggplant will absorb any oil you put in. Then set eggplant aside on paper towel to drain. Repeat with potatoes. In large baking dish, layer potatoes, meat sauce, and eggplant. Prepare a thick Bechamel (white sauce): Melt butter, add flour slowly, and stir. Then add hot milk, salt, pepper and nutmeg. Cook a few minutes on very low heat, stirring continuously, and then remove pan. Add eggs and cheese and stir. Spread over casserole. Bake at 350° for about 45 minutes or until golden. Serves 6.

Sun Line Cruises

Shrimp à la Mikrolimano

1¼ pounds shrimp, peeled and deveined
1 carrot
1 small onion
1 small green pepper, seeded
4 stalks celery, with leaves
3 medium tomatoes, peeled and seeded, or a 16 ounce can whole tomatoes
1 tablespoon butter
⅓ cup white wine
1 teaspoon oregano
Salt and pepper to taste
6 ounces feta cheese, crumbled
4 ounces Parmesan cheese, grated

Finely chop carrot, onion, green pepper, celery and tomatoes. Reserve tomatoes and sauté other vegetables in medium-sized saucepan with half the butter until onion is golden. Remove vegetables and in same pan melt remaining butter. When bubbling, add whole shrimp, stirring for 2 to 3 minutes. Add wine and cook on medium heat. Return vegetables to pan. Add tomatoes. Add oregano, salt and pepper. Scoop about 5 shrimp with vegetables into individual ramekins or put entire contents into a baking dish. Sprinkle with feta and top with Parmesan. Place dish or ramekins in a very hot oven for 5 minutes. Serve at once. Serves 6.

Baklava with Walnuts and Almonds

For baklava pastry:

    1 pound filo (sold in delicatessens)
    1½ cups almonds, finely chopped
    1½ cups walnuts, finely chopped
    Cinnamon
    2 cups unsalted butter, melted

For syrup:

    2 cups sugar
    1½ cups water
    1 teaspoon ground cloves
    1 tablespoon cinnamon
    1 cinnamon stick
    ½ cup honey
    3 tablespoons orange peel
    3 tablespoons lemon peel

To prepare baklava pastry: Grind nuts and sprinkle them with cinnamon. Grease bottom of large baking dish well and put in 2 sheets of filo. Brush sheets with butter and cover surface with nuts. Continue to layer sheets in this manner until all nuts are used. Finish top with 8 to 10 sheets of filo only. With sharp knife, score baklava in diamond or square shapes, cutting through bottom layer. Bake in very slow oven, 250°, for 2 hours or until golden. Remove from oven and allow to cool completely.

To prepare syrup: Put sugar and water in pan and bring to a boil for 5 minutes. Add cloves, cinnamon, cinnamon

Sun Line Cruises

stick, honey, and lemon and orange peel. Boil for 5 minutes longer. Pour hot syrup onto cold baklava. Cool and cut through layers again. Note: always pour hot syrup on cold baklava, never hot on hot.

Eggplant Imam

2 large eggplants
2 onions
4 cloves garlic, crushed
4 tablespoons parsley, finely chopped
1 pound fresh, ripe tomatoes, sliced
1 cup olive oil
½ teaspoon cumin seed
1 dash sugar
Salt and pepper to taste

Cut each eggplant into quarters. Remove seeds, if any. Salt and let stand 15 to 20 minutes in water. Wash well and dry with paper towels. Fry in hot oil until soft. Drain excess oil. Place in baking dish and make indentation in center of each. Sauté well all other ingredients except tomatoes. Stuff each eggplant and top with 1 or 2 slices tomato. Bake in a moderate oven of 350° for about 30 to 40 minutes. Serves 4.

Walnut and Almond Cake

For syrup:

    3 cups water
    2 cinnamon sticks
    1 slice lemon
    1 cup honey
    1 cup sugar
    ½ cup rum or cognac
    Peel of orange or lemon

For batter:

    ½ pound butter, softened
    1 cup sugar
    6 eggs
    1 cup flour, sifted
    1 cup farina or semolina
    2 heaping teaspoons baking powder
    1 teaspoon cinnamon
    1 tablespoon orange peel, grated
    1 cup nuts, finely chopped

To prepare syrup: Combine all ingredients in saucepan. Boil for 10 minutes. Set aside to cool.

To prepare batter: Cream butter and sugar until very light. Add eggs, one at a time, beating constantly. Add flour, farina or semolina, baking powder, cinnamon and orange peel, and beat well. Add nuts and mix thoroughly. Pour batter into a 9 by 13 inch buttered pan and bake at 350° for 30 minutes. Pour cooled syrup over cake. Allow to cool and cut into diamond shapes. Serves 6.

Chapter Five

Presidential Nile Cruises

Just like Cleopatra, today's traveler can spend a luxurious vacation cruising the Nile River in Egypt. More sumptuous than Queen Cleopatra's barge are the four ships of the Presidential Nile Cruises Lines: the Nile Princess, Nile Emperor, Nile President and Nile Legend. All ships make five to eleven day trips from Cairo, Luxor and Aswan.

The Nile Emperor sails past an Egyptian backdrop.

Cruise Ship Cookbook

Stops along the way include visits to the tomb of King Tutankhamen, the temples at Karnak and Luxor, the pyramids, Elephantine Island and many more sites of ancient Egypt.

But shipboard life offers more enchantments than the magnificent remains of a 5000-year-old civilization. You can bask in the hot Egyptian sun, have a dip in the ship's large pool, watch belly dancers at the bar, relax on the deck as the picturesque life along the banks of the Nile sweeps by. Or you can eat, eat, eat!

The food aboard the Presidential Nile cruise ships is, quite literally, fit for a king. In fact, the ships have often hosted ambassadors, kings and queens. A French food and beverage manager—as well as an Egyptian chef—supervises the meals.

The predominant theme is Middle Eastern gourmet, best exhibited one night of each cruise when a special "Egyptian Evening" is organized. Classic Arabian dishes appear on the buffet table that night, including the perennial passenger favorites that are featured here:

Kunafah
(Shredded Pastry with Nuts and Syrup)

For syrup:

>   1¾ cups sugar
>   12 fluid ounces water
>   Juice of 1 lemon
>   1 tablespoon orange blossom water, available in specialty stores

For pastry:

>1 pound kunafah pastry (usually 1 packet, available in specialty stores)
>¾ pound unsalted butter, melted and with froth removed
>12 ounces pistachio nuts, whole
>3 tablespoons sugar
>3 ounces almonds, finely chopped

To prepare syrup: Put sugar, water and lemon juice into a saucepan and bring it to a boil. Lower heat and simmer until syrup begins to leave sticky film on spoon. Remove from heat. Stir in orange blossom water and set aside to cool.

To prepare pastry: Preheat oven to 180°. Put pastry into large bowl and ease apart strands, gently to avoid breakage. Divide pastry into 3 portions. Take 1 portion and lay it flat on a clean working top. With pastry brush, coat surface with some of melted butter. Take a flat stick, about 18 inches long, and lay it diagonally across flattened pastry. Mix pistachio nuts with sugar and almonds and arrange a third of filling evenly along stick. Roll strands of dough around stick as tightly as possible. Carefully slide stick out, leaving filling inside. Brush melted butter all over roll of pastry. Prepare other portions of pastry in same way. Arrange pastry rolls in tin and bake for 30 minutes. Lower heat to 150° and bake for 1½ more hours until golden brown. Remove from oven and pour cold syrup over rolls, turning each so it is covered completely. Let cool. Cut each roll into 2 to 3 inch pieces. Makes 3 dozen.

Hummus−Bi−Tahina

This appetizer can be served as a vegetable dip or as a side dish. It has a marvellous aroma and blends extremely well with most meat dishes, especially shish kebab.

> 1 pound chickpeas, soaked in cold water overnight
> 1 teaspoon baking soda
> 3 cloves garlic, peeled
> 1 cup tahini paste
> 1 teaspoon chili powder
> 3 teaspoons salt
> 2 teaspoons cumin
> Juice of 2 to 3 lemons

For garnish—a little of each:

> Red pepper
> Cumin
> Lemon juice
> Olive oil
> Parsley, chopped

Place drained chickpeas and baking soda in large saucepan, filled ¾ full with water. Bring to a boil. Lower heat and simmer until chickpeas are tender, removing surface scum from time to time and adding more boiling water if necessary. Drain chickpeas into sieve and rinse very thoroughly under cold water. Set aside a few whole chickpeas to use as garnish. Reduce remainder to a thick paste or purée. A food processor is fine for this purpose. While liquidizing the chickpeas, add cloves garlic. This will ensure that they are properly ground. Empty purée into large bowl. Add all remaining ingredients and mix thoroughly. Taste and adjust seasoning to your liking. Serve in a star pattern. Pour a little olive oil and lemon juice in center. Serves 6.

Daoud Pasha
(Meatballs and Pine Nuts Coated with Tomato Sauce)

This is a very rich dish, best served with plain rice. The tasty meal is dedicated to Garabed Artin Pasha Daoudian, an Armenian who became the first governor of Lebanon and the first Christian to hold such a high office in the Ottoman Empire.

1 pound lamb, minced
1 teaspoon salt
¼ teaspoon black pepper
½ teaspoon cumin
1 teaspoon coriander
½ teaspoon allspice
2 tablespoons olive oil
1 onion, thinly sliced
2 tablespoons pine nuts or blanched almonds
2 tablespoons tomato purée
1 tablespoon lemon juice
½ tablespoon dried basil
1 tablespoon butter

In large bowl, mix together meat, salt, pepper, cumin, ½ teaspoon coriander and allspice. Shape mixture into small balls. Heat olive oil in saucepan. Add onion and cook until soft and lightly colored. Add meatballs and fry for 10 minutes. Add pine nuts and fry for 2 minutes more. Pour in diluted tomato purée and lemon juice and add basil and remaining coriander. Stir well to coat meatballs with mixture. Reduce heat to low and simmer for 30 minutes. Transfer meatballs and sauce to a warmed serving dish and keep hot. Melt butter in a small frying pan. Add remaining pine nuts and cook for a few minutes until golden. Place one nut in each meatball and serve at once. Serves 6.

Sayyadeya
(Fish with Rice)

This is a traditional dish cooked by fishermen. They consider it a soup.

For fish:

- 2 pounds halibut steaks, halved
- 2 tablespoons butter
- 2 tablespoons lemon juice
- ½ teaspoon salt
- ¼ teaspoon black pepper
- 2 tablespoons parsley, chopped

Presidential Nile Cruises

For stew:

    6 tablespoons olive oil
    1 onion, finely chopped
    2 tablespoons pine nuts
    1 tablespoon raisins
    ½ teaspoon allspice
    Saffron rice, as much as desired
    2 tablespoons lemon juice
    2 tablespoons parsley, chopped
    1 teaspoon salt
    ½ teaspoon black pepper

For sauce:

    4 tablespoons olive oil
    1 tablespoon pine nuts
    1 tablespoon dried mint
    1 tablespoon lemon juice
    ½ teaspoon cumin

To prepare fish: Preheat oven to 180°. Melt 1 tablespoon butter in large shallow baking dish and add pieces of fish. Sprinkle with salt, pepper, lemon juice and parsley. Dot remaining butter over fish. Bake until fish flakes easily. Set aside.

To prepare stew: In large saucepan, heat oil and sauté onion until soft. Add nuts, raisins, allspice, and saffron rice. Also add lemon juice, parsley, salt and pepper and mix well. Remove fish from baking dish. Spread half of rice mixture over base of baking dish. Layer half of fish on top. Add a layer of rice and top with remaining fish.

To prepare sauce: Heat oil in pan. Add nuts, mint, lemon juice and cumin. Cook for 5 minutes and pour over baking dish. Bake 15 minutes at 180°. Serve at once. Serves 6.

Chapter Six

Home Lines

Sail away on a vacation more comfortable, more relaxing than just staying at home. Home Lines, cruising the Caribbean, offers food, service and accomodations in the best Mediterranean tradition. On both the M.V. Homeric and the M.V. Atlantic, the all-Italian staff is eager to please you: the stewards make a special point of learning your name and your waiter will know your favorite drink in no time. Delicious Italian cuisine is available non-stop, from espresso and fresh juice in your cabin when you wake, to hot pizza at 2:00 a.m.

The M.V. Homeric made its maiden voyage in 1986.

Cruise Ship Cookbook

You won't get a chance to participate in all the activities available aboard these ships—not unless you pass up your chance to visit the lovely Caribbean ports. So pick your favorites: swim, visit the gym, or play a relaxing game of backgammon or bingo. Attend mini-courses where you'll learn to play bridge, improve your golf game or speak Italian. See a fashion show and visit the soda fountain in the afternoon, and spend the evening dancing in the disco or ballroom. Tomorrow night, for variety, you can try your luck at the casino or visit the movie theatre.

The ship is so much a home away from home that you may feel a bit reluctant to leave it to visit the casinos of San Juan and Nassau, pirates' coves of St. Thomas, and wonderful half French, half Dutch St. Maarten. Highlights of your trip might include the birthplace of Napoleon's Empress Josephine in Martinique, 19th century castles of Barbados, and Mayan ruins of Cozumel.

It's hard to resist having your dinner aboard the ship, though. Sixty master chefs, cooks, bakers and pastrymen work together to create a different eight-course meal every evening. You'll enjoy French night, Bermuda night and, of course, Home Line's specialty, Italian night. Some of the favorites are featured here:

Frozen Imperial

1 ounce orange juice
1½ ounces Galliano

Mix in blender with scoops of shaved ice. Decorate with maraschino cherry and a few drops of grenadine syrup.

Home Lines

Oceanic Special

1½ ounces Bacardi
1½ ounces pineapple juice
¼ ounce grapefruit juice
2 dashes grenadine syrup
2 dashes dry martini vermouth
2 dashes Galliano

Combine ingredients and shake with ice. Decorate with maraschino cherry and a slice of orange.

Homeric Special

1½ ounces Bacardi rum
1½ ounces pineapple juice
¼ ounce grapefruit juice
2 dashes dry martini vermouth
2 dashes grenadine syrup
1 dash Galliano

Combine ingredients and shake with ice. Decorate with maraschino cherry and slice of orange.

Peach Bellini

⅓ part peach and black currant nectar
⅔ part chilled champagne

Pour ingredients in a champagne glass and stir.

Yellow Bird

1½ ounces orange juice
1½ ounces gin
¾ ounce Galliano

Combine ingredients and shake with ice. Decorate with maraschino cherry and a slice of orange.

Piña Colada

2 ounces pineapple juice
½ ounce cream of coconut
2 ounces white rum

Mix ingredients in blender with cracked ice. Decorate with maraschino cherry.

Portofino

1 ounce orange juice
½ ounce lemon juice
1½ ounces gin
1½ ounces Galliano
¼ ounce peppermint

Combine ingredients and shake with ice. Decorate with maraschino cherry and a slice of orange.

Pineapple Tropical Night Dream

1 large pineapple
1 pound strawberries
3 tablespoons sugar
2 small glass maraschino liqueur
6 egg yolks
3 ounces sugar
½ cup fine cherry liqueur

Cut pineapple 2 inches under foliage to make a vase and cover. Very carefully, without breaking the outside, remove pineapple pulp. Refrigerate empty vase. Dice pulp and strawberries. Place in bowl and add sugar and 1 glass maraschino liqueur. Stir and place in refrigerator to cool. In pan, beat egg yolks, sugar, fine cherry liqueur and remaining maraschino liqueur. Add pineapple pulp-strawberry mixture and stir. Fill empty vase. Cover vase with foliage to reform the pineapple. Serve well chilled.

Tricolor

Juice of ½ lemon
½ teaspoon sugar
1½ ounces vodka
2 dashes grenadine
2 dashes kiwi syrup

Mix lemon, sugar and vodka in blender with cracked ice. Serve in tall glass. Put grenadine and kiwi syrup on opposite sides of glass.

Lasagne Verdi al Forno "Gastronomica"

2 pounds flour
4 eggs
1 spinach, cooked, chopped and well drained
2 tablespoons butter
2 tablespoons flour
1 cup milk
Parmesan cheese, grated
Sausage, cut in small pieces
Mushrooms, fresh, browned in butter

To prepare lasagne pasta: Mix flour, eggs and spinach into a well blended paste. Roll out into a thin sheet and cut into 4 inch squares. Drop them into cold water and drain. Spread on damp towels.

To prepare cream sauce: Melt butter in saucepan. Add flour and stir. Add milk and heat, stirring until creamy.

Butter large baking dish and coat bottom with half of cream sauce. Layer lasagne pasta over this. Sprinkle with parmesan cheese, sausage and mushroom. Continue to add layers until dish is filled. Coat top with cream sauce, parmesan cheese and a little butter. Bake at 375° for 15 minutes or until all layers of cheese are melted.

Delight of Shrimp "Las Vegas"

2 pounds shrimp, shelled, deveined and rinsed
Salt and pepper to taste
Flour, as needed
1 tablespoon olive oil
2 ounces butter
½ tablespoon onion, finely chopped
½ tablespoon leek, finely chopped
1 small glass whiskey
1 glass Madeira
4 egg yolks
6 ounces cream
Cayenne pepper to taste
1 dash tarragon

Season shrimp with salt and pepper and powder with flour. In pan, heat olive oil and butter. Add shrimp and stir gently until they have a lively, red color. Add onion and leek. Add whisky and light contents of pan. After flame has subsided, pour in Madeira and let cook for 15 minutes. In another pan, beat egg yolks, cream, cayenne pepper and tarragon. Stir and pour over shrimp. Serve with golden fleurons or soda crackers.

Lobster Virgin Islands

2 lobsters, live
2 ounces sweet butter
½ cup olive oil
3 small glasses cognac
1 glass white wine
2 pounds tomatoes, peeled and mashed
1 tablespoon leek, chopped
2 cloves garlic
½ leaf laurel
1 small bunch tarragon
1 dash cayenne pepper
½ cup heavy cream
1 pound mushrooms, thinly sliced
Butter, as needed

Remove heads of live lobsters and open them vertically. Cut tails in 1 inch pieces and crush claws in order to remove (when cooked) in 1 piece. In pan, melt sweet butter. Add olive oil, lobster, 2 small glasses cognac, white wine, tomatoes, leek, 1 garlic clove and laurel. Finely chop 1 teaspoon tarragon and reserve. Add remainder to pan. Cover pan and let contents cook for 35 minutes. Add only sufficient water to keep from burning. When cooked, take out lobster piece by piece and keep in warm place. Strain rest of contents and put back in pan to cook. Add remaining glass of cognac, teaspoon tarragon, cayenne pepper and heavy cream. Heat without boiling. Sauté mushrooms in butter with remaining clove garlic. Stir mushrooms into sauce. Pour sauce over lobster. Serve with buttered rice.

Bolognese Meat Sauce

2 tablespoons butter
1 cup bacon, diced small
½ cup ham, diced small
2 medium onions, finely chopped
2 carrots, finely chopped
2 stalks celery, finely chopped
½ pound beef, finely chopped
1 pound veal, finely chopped
1 pound pork, finely chopped
Dry red wine, as desired
2 tablespoons tomato paste
2 bay leaves
1 teaspoon salt
Pepper, freshly ground, to taste
5 cloves
1 dash nutmeg
½ pound mushrooms, sliced
4 chicken livers, diced

Melt butter in pan and brown bacon and ham. Add onions, carrots and celery. When vegetables have softened, add beef, veal and pork. Stir and partially cook meat. Add wine. Simmer mixture until wine has almost evaporated. Add tomato paste, bay leaves, salt, pepper, cloves, nutmeg and enough hot water to almost cover ingredients. Cover pan and let sauce simmer slowly for about 2 hours. Add mushrooms and chicken livers and cook for 15 minutes longer. Sauce should be thick when served.

Saltimbocca alla Romana

8 small veal scallops
Salt and pepper to taste
8 small leaves sage, fresh
8 thin slices *prosciutto* (Italian ham), size of veal scallops
3 tablespoons butter, melted
Wine, as needed

Flatten veal scallops until they are less than ¼ inch thick. Season with salt and pepper. To each scallop, add a leaf sage and a slice *prosciutto*. Fasten veal and *prosciutto* together with wooden toothpicks threaded through the meat. Sauté meat in butter for about 10 minutes, lightly on *prosciutto* side, more thoroughly on veal side. Remove toothpicks. Arrange on hot platter. Deglaze pan with a little wine and pour sauce over meat. Serve with artichokes fried in butter.

Scaloppine di Tacchino Reale

Turkey breast, sliced very thin
Flour
Butter
1 tablespoon olive oil
Salt and pepper to taste
Cherry brandy
Tomatoes, ripe, chopped to a thick purée
Mushrooms, finely chopped
Worcestershire sauce to taste
½ lemon
Parsley, finely chopped

Dust both sides of turkey breast with flour and place in pan with a little butter and olive oil. Sprinkle with salt and pepper. Flame with some cherry brandy. Spread tomatoes and mushrooms over turkey breast. Sprinkle with worcestershire sauce and a little more cherry brandy. Cook a few minutes until sauce reaches desired consistency. Squeeze lemon over turkey breast and garnish with parsley.

Chicken alla Cacciatora

1 small chicken
Flour
Salt and pepper to taste
2 tablespoons olive oil
2 tablespoons butter
1 onion, chopped
1 bunch aromatic herb
½ glass dry white wine
1½ cup fresh mushrooms, sliced
3 tomatoes, peeled, seeded and coarsely chopped
1 tablespoon parsley, minced
3 cups any stock

Cut chicken into 4 pieces and remove bones. Dust it with flour and season it with salt and pepper. In heavy pan, brown chicken pieces on all sides in butter and olive oil. Add onion and aromatic herb. Add white wine and simmer until it evaporates, approximately 10 minutes. Add mushrooms, tomatoes, parsley and stock. Cover pan and simmer 45 minutes or until almost tender. Add small quantities of hot water if necessary.

Ossobuco Milanese Style

The chefs of Home Lines recommend that you serve this well known dish with Golden risotto.

Hollowbone
Flour
Salt to taste
White wine to taste
1 cup beef stock
Parsley to taste
Garlic to taste
Lemon peel as desired
Anchovies as desired

Roll hollowbone in flour, sprinkle with salt, and brown well in skillet. Add white wine and simmer. When wine is evaporated, add beef stock. Cover skillet and cook for 1 hour. Add parsley, garlic, lemon peel and anchovies and cook for 15 more minutes. Place bones in serving dish. Pour sauce over them and serve.

Dolce Monte Bianco
(Chestnut Pie)

6 pounds chestnuts
4 tablespoons butter
6 ounces sugar
1 small glass Jamaican rum
2 glasses Sandeman (port wine)
Whipped cream
Glazed chestnuts

Peel off first skin of chestnuts and boil them in a little salted water. When cooked, peel off inner skin and clean them well. Place in bowl and add butter, sugar, rum and Sandeman. Mix contents well, reducing them to paste. On plate, mold paste to form a cone. Cover cone with whipped cream. To garnish, circle cone with glazed chestnuts. Chill 1 hour and serve.

Crepes Lady Wonderful Caprice

Pre-made crepes
3 bananas, peeled
3 tablespoons sugar
1 tablespoon banana liqueur
5 preserved kumquats, diced
Butter
Confectioner's sugar
Brandy

Purée bananas and strain. Add sugar, banana liqueur and kumquats. Mix thoroughly. Spread thin coat over crepes and roll them. Cover bottom of chafing dish with a very thin layer of butter. Arrange crepes in dish and sprinkle them with confectioner's sugar. Flame with brandy and serve immediately.

Part Three
A Taste of Europe

Chapter Seven

Premier Cruise Lines

Sleek and clean of line like a greyhound, with nautical flags strung from bow to stern, the S.S. Royale, with her bold, scarlet hull, is an exceptionally striking sight as she moves through the water—a kaleidoscope of color. The Royale of the Premier Cruise Line specializes in three and four day cruises from Central Florida to Nassau and the Out Islands.

Goombay music, Calypso dancing, horse racing, handwriting analyses, sing-alongs and fashion shows are some of the activities that will occupy your shipboard hours in between lavish and innovative dining.

Each cruise uses 320 gallons of ice cream, 5300 pounds of meat, 18,000 eggs and 3000 pounds of vegetables. This tremendous amount of food is used to prepare meals for the elegant dining room, which transforms from a French bistro to an Italian café to a Caribbean nightclub to a Stars 'n Stripes banquet. The motif is determined by the dinner theme of the evening.

According to Executive Chef Francisco Estrada, Caterer Apollo, and the kitchen staff of 100, whatever the language, the accent is on superb dining.

Premier Cruise Lines

Crepes St. Michel

12 crepes (make ones from following recipe or buy frozen from gourmet section of supermarket)
½ cup butter
3 or more tablespoons flour, as needed
1 cup milk
1 cup heavy cream
3 ounces bacon, diced small
2 ounces onions, chopped
3 ounces ham, diced small
1 cup spinach, finely chopped and cooked
3 ounces Swiss cheese, diced small
1 egg yolk
1 teaspoon lemon juice
2 tablespoons sherry
Salt, pepper and nutmeg to taste
Parmesan cheese, grated, as needed

First make a cream sauce: In saucepan, melt 6 tablespoons butter. Add flour, cook a few minutes, and whip in milk and cream. Simmer 2 minutes. You should have about 2 cups of cream sauce. Now, in frying pan, cook bacon crisp. Drain, and save bacon fat for other purposes. Cook onions in 2 tablespoons of butter until done but not brown. Add ham and continue cooking. Then add spinach, Swiss cheese and bacon, and cook 2 more minutes. Add 1 cup cream sauce and bring to a good boil. Use this mixture to fill crepes. Roll up crepes and line buttered casserole with them. Take remaining cup of cream sauce and add egg yolk, lemon juice, nutmeg, salt and pepper. Pour this sauce over crepes, and sprinkle them generously with parmesan cheese. Brown in 400° oven. Serve piping hot.

Crepes

1 cup milk, room temperature
2 eggs
¼ teaspoon salt
1 cup flour
2 tablespoons butter, melted

Beat all ingredients by hand or use food processor. Strain and let stand in refrigerator for 2 hours. Heat slightly greased, non-stick pan. Pour small amount crepe of batter into pan. Do not turn crepe. Turn pan so that bottom is covered. When done, slide off pan and pour excess batter into mixture. Use filling of your choice or follow previous recipe. Serves 4 to 6.

Cold Cucumber Soup

This recipe may be made with a food processor.

3 medium or 2 large cucumbers, peeled and grated
2 tablespoons onions, grated
2 tablespoons dill, minced
1 tablespoon parsley, minced
Sliced toasted almonds, as needed
1½ cups sour cream
½ to ¾ cup buttermilk
6 extra slices cucumber, marinated in vinegar
Salt and pepper to taste
Worcestershire sauce to taste

Combine sour cream and buttermilk with salt, pepper and worcestershire sauce. Add cucumbers, then onions, then parsley and dill. Serve in chilled cups. Sprinkle with almonds and place a slice of cucumber on top. Serves 6.

Chilled Strawberry Soup

>1 pound strawberries, frozen
>Juice of 1 lemon
>1 or 2 pieces lemon peel
>2 tablespoons cornstarch
>½ cup sweet red wine
>½ cup sour cream
>½ cup cream

For garnish:

>Fresh strawberries
>Confectioner's sugar
>Cointreau
>Mint leaves

Drain strawberries into pan. Boil syrup from strawberries with enough water to make 2 cups. Add lemon juice and peel. Simmer for 2 minutes. Dissolve cornstarch in some red wine and add to soup. Stir continuously as it thickens. Let cool. Purée strawberries in blender or food processor. Add to soup together with red wine, sour cream and cream. Serve in chilled cups. To garnish, dip strawberries in cointreau and confectioner's sugar. A sprig of mint looks nice on top. Serves 4 to 6.

Poached Filet of Sole al Aguacate

For poaching liquid:

    2 cups water
    1 lemon
    1 bay leaf
    Salt and pepper to taste

For fish and sauce:

    1½ pounds sole filets
    1 cup avocado pulp (make in food processor or buy canned or frozen)
    Maggi seasoning to taste
    Worcestershire sauce to taste
    1 or 2 jalapeno peppers, finely minced
    1 tablespoon coriander, chopped or dried
    ½ cup heavy cream

For garnish:

    8 tomato slices
    8 hard boiled egg slices
    8 lime wedges
    Shredded lettuce as needed

Combine ingredients of poaching liquid. Poach sole filets in poaching liquid. Cool filets and refrigerate. Combine sauce ingredients with avocado pulp and season to taste. Place fish on shredded lettuce. Coat with avocado sauce and garnish with tomato, hard boiled eggs and lime wedges. Serves 4 to 6.

Insalata De Calamari
(Squid Appetizer)

1 pound squid, fresh or frozen
Salt and pepper to taste
3 tablespoons onions, coarsely chopped
½ teaspoon garlic, finely chopped
2 tablespoons fresh dill, chopped
2 tablespoons parsley, chopped
1 tablespoon basil if fresh or ½ tablespoon dry
¾ cup olive oil
¼ cup wine vinegar
5 thin slices lemon

For garnish, use any or all of the following:

Whole lettuce leaves
Green pepper rings
Tomato wedges
Hard boiled egg wedges
Red onion rings
Capers

Cook squid in boiling water for about 15 minutes or until cooked. Strain and let cool. Remove any transparent cartilage and cut into ½ inch strips. Sprinkle with salt, pepper, onions and garlic. Add other ingredients, including lemon slices. Marinate in a covered container for 1 day minimum. Place in lettuce cup and garnish.

Pineapple Torte

1½ cups almond paste (available in gourmet section of supermarket)
1¼ cups egg whites
1 cup sugar
1½ ounces cornstarch
2½ ounces cake crumbs (from stale cake or cookies)
½ yellow cake mix
Milk, ½ amount suggested on cake mix package directions
1 orange, grated
1 cup pineapple paste (finely chop crushed or canned pineapple or mash fresh pineapple in food processor)
2 cups heavy whipped cream

To prepare first layer: Soften almond paste with ½ cup egg whites. Blend in ½ cup sugar and whip until smooth. You may use a food processor. Whip remaining amount of egg whites until stiff and add to mixture. Also add cornstarch and cake crumbs. Bake in greased and floured 8 inch cake pan at 375° for 30 minutes.

To prepare second layer: Add milk, orange and ½ cup pineapple paste to cake mix. Bake the same way.

Whip cream and combine remaining pineapple paste and sugar. Use some of this topping to put layers together. Use some to spread on top. Divide into 8 to 10 portions. Put rosette of whipped cream on each slice and decorate with glazed or canned pineapple. Serves 8 to 10.

Premier Cruise Lines

Filet of Sole Marguery

2½ pounds filet of sole or any other white meat fish
2 shallots, chopped
2 cups fish stock or clam juice
1 cup white wine
2 bay leaves
½ lemon, sliced
Salt to taste
Cayenne pepper or hot sauce to taste
3 tablespoons butter, softened
2 to 3 tablespoons flour, as needed
2 egg yolks
1 tablespoon lemon juice
6 to 12 oysters, poached
12 shrimp, cooked
12 scallops, cooked (optional)

Sprinkle shallots over bottom of a buttered pan or casserole. Line up filets (if too thin, fold them). Cover with fish stock or clam juice, white wine, bay leaves, sliced lemon, salt and cayenne pepper. Cover pan tightly and cook for about 10 minutes on top of stove until done. Drain most of juice into saucepan. Remove bay leaves. Make a roux out of butter and flour and whip into fish stock. Bring this sauce to a boil, adding more wine if necessary. Remove from stove immediately. Beat egg yolks and lemon juice into boiling sauce. Place filets in ovenproof dish. Decorate each with 1 or 2 poached oysters, shrimp and scallops. Coat filets with sauce. Glaze under broiler or in hot oven. Serves 6 or more.

Cruise Ship Cookbook

Apollo Pork Loin

5 pounds pork loin, center cut
½ cup pineapple juice
⅓ cup mango nectar
Handful parsley stems
2 teaspoons garlic, chopped
2 teaspoons chives
2 tablespoons cider vinegar
1 tablespoon worcestershire sauce
½ cup white wine
½ cup orange juice
1 teaspoon whole cloves
1 teaspoon dry English mustard
1 teaspoon turmeric
Salt and pepper to taste
1 cup carrots, coarsely chopped
1 cup onions, coarsely chopped
1 cup celery, coarsely chopped

Make a marinade of pineapple juice, mango nectar, parsley stems, garlic, chives, vinegar, worcestershire sauce, white wine, orange juice, cloves, mustard and turmeric. Season pork loin lightly with salt and pepper. Pour marinade over pork. Refrigerate overnight in closed container. The next day, roast pork, carrots, onions and celery in roasting pan about 1½ hours or until done. While roasting, baste pork and vegetables periodically with marinade. When done, keep roast hot and deglaze roasting pan. Use all drippings and vegetables to make sauce and add some white wine and water. Boil for a few minutes and strain. If sauce requires thickening, you may add arrowroot or cornstarch, dissolved in white wine. Slice pork loin and serve with some fried plantains or bananas, beans and rice, or your favorite fruit stuffing. Serves 6 or more.

Baked Stuffed Potatoes

4 Idaho potatoes
1½ cups hot milk
2 tablespoons butter
4 ounces bacon, crisp and finely chopped
2 to 3 tablespoons scallions, finely chopped
Salt and pepper to taste
Nutmeg to taste
Parmesan cheese, grated, as needed
Paprika, as needed

Bake potatoes in 450° oven for 50 minutes. Cut in half and scoop most of the potato out, leaving 8 shells. Whip scooped out potatoes (a food processor may be used). Add all other ingredients except parmesan cheese and paprika and correct seasoning. Spoon or pipe potatoes back into shells. All shells need not be used. Top with parmesan cheese and paprika and brown in hot oven for 5 minutes. Serves 4 to 6.

Coquille of Curried Seafood

This dish is served as an appetizer on the Dolphin, but you may serve it as a main course.

For curry sauce:

> ½ cup onions, finely chopped
> ¼ cup celery, finely chopped
> ¼ cup green apples, finely chopped
> ½ cup butter
> 1 cup flour
> 2 to 3 tablespoons curry powder
> 2 cups hot milk
> 2 bay leaves
> 4 peppercorns
> Nutmeg to taste
> Worcestershire sauce to taste
> Salt and pepper to taste
> 1 tablespoon lemon juice

Dine in elegance aboard the S.S. Royale.

Premier Cruise Lines

For Duchess potatoes:

> Potatoes, as needed
> Milk, as needed
> 1 tablespoon butter
> 2 egg yolks
> Salt and pepper to taste
> Nutmeg to taste

For seafood:

> 20 ounces of seafood, (scallops, lobster, shrimp, crab meat, flaked fish)
> 3 ounces butter
> ¼ cup sherry
> 2 cups curry sauce
> ½ cup heavy cream
> ½ cup tomatoes

To prepare curry sauce: Sauté onions, celery and green apples in a little butter until cooked but not brown. Stir in remaining butter, flour and curry powder, and cook for 3 minutes more. Stir in hot milk and remaining ingredients. Simmer for 20 minutes, stirring occasionally.

To prepare Duchess potatoes: Make about 2 cups stiffly mashed potatoes, using a spare amount of milk. Whip in butter and 2 egg yolks. Add salt, pepper and nutmeg.

To prepare seafood: Sauté seafood in butter. Add sherry and curry sauce. Simmer 40 minutes. Add heavy cream and tomatoes. Adjust seasoning. Pipe fancy border of Duchess potatoes around 4 to 6 small casseroles, ramekins or baking shells. Fill casseroles with seafood mixture.

Gebratener Kapaun auf Wildbret Art
(Capon or Roasting Chicken in the Style of Game)

1 capon or roasting chicken
Salt and pepper to taste
2 carrots, coarsely chopped
2 stalks celery, coarsely chopped
2 onions, coarsely chopped
2 cloves garlic, finely chopped
½ cup oil
1 cup Madeira or sherry
2 tablespoons pickling spice
2 tablespoons juniper berries, crushed
⅓ cup wine vinegar
¼ cup white wine
½ cup currant jelly
1 cup sour cream
Cornstarch, as needed for thickening

Season chicken inside and out with salt and pepper. Place in bowl with carrots, celery and onions. Make a marinade of garlic, oil, Madeira or sherry, pickling spices, juniper berries and wine vinegar. Pour over chicken and vegetables. Let stand at least 1 hour, basting periodically. Roast chicken at 400°, basting frequently. Chicken will be done in 3 hours or when juices from chicken run clear. Remove chicken and vegetables to large platter. Pour roasting juices into saucepan. Deglaze roasting pan with ¼ cup white wine and water. Put contents in saucepan and simmer for 20 minutes. Add currant jelly. Strain. Mix sour cream with cornstarch and a little warm sauce. Add to remainder of sauce. Slice chicken and arrange with vegetables on platter. Good with noodles. Serves 4 to 6.

Veal Scallops Valle d'Auge

For cream sauce:

    ½ cup hot milk
    1½ tablespoons butter
    1 tablespoon flour

For veal:

    8 to 10 small veal cutlets
    Salt and pepper to taste
    ¾ cup herb seasoning
    ⅓ cup onions, chopped
    1 cup calvados or applejack
    ½ cup cream sauce
    ½ cup heavy cream
    ½ cup Chablis
    2 carrots, cut into 1 by ½ inch batonettes
    2 turnips, cut into 1 by ½ inch batonettes
    ½ cup green beans, fresh or frozen
    ½ cup green peas, fresh or frozen
    ¼ cup butter
    1 cup flour
    ¾ cup milk

To prepare cream sauce: Melt butter. Stir in flour. Add hot milk. Simmer until thickened, stirring continuously.

To prepare veal: Season meat with salt, pepper and herb seasoning. Sauté cutlets in a little butter and/or oil. Add onions and then calvados or applejack. Flame it at this stage. Add cream sauce, cream and Chablis, and bring it to a boil. In separate pan, blanch remaining vegetables in lightly salted water until cooked yet crisp. Add vegetables to meat. In saucepan, melt butter and add flour to make a roux. Whip moderately warm milk into mixture. Continue heating, stirring until smooth. It should be thick when it comes to a boil. Pour over veal cutlets. Simmer for 30 minutes. Serves 4 to 6.

Carrots Veronique

1 pound fresh carrots, peeled and cut into 1 by ½ inch batonettes (frozen baby carrots may be substituted)
¼ cup onions, finely chopped
2 tablespoons butter
1½ cups chicken stock
Salt to taste
1 to 2 tablespoons sugar
Chives, chopped, as needed

Cook onions in butter for 10 minutes until done but not brown. Add chicken stock, carrots and other ingredients. Cover and simmer until carrots are done. This process should reduce the liquid so that carrots are glazed. Serves 4 to 6.

Premier Cruise Lines

Beef Bourguignonne

2½ pounds beef sirloin tips
2 ounces salt pork or bacon, diced
⅛ cup onions, chopped
Herb seasoning to taste
Salt and pepper to taste
1 cup red wine
1 cup tomato purée
½ cup brown sauce
½ pound mushrooms, sliced
Lemon juice to taste
1 small can pearl onions
2 tablespoons liver or veal pâté, diced (optional)
Arrowroot or cornstarch, as needed for thickening

Sauté beef tips in a little oil and/or butter. Sauté salt pork until lightly browned. Discard fat. Combine with beef tips. Add chopped onions, herb seasoning, salt and pepper. Cook for 10 minutes. Add wine, tomato purée and brown sauce to meat. Simmer for 20 minutes. Meanwhile, blanch mushrooms in boiling salted water with lemon juice. Drain and add these and pearl onions to meat. Bring to a good boil. The pâté can be added at this point. If too thin, add a little arrowroot or cornstarch dissolved in red wine. Serve over noodles, rice or in pastry shells. Serves 4 to 6.

Chapter Eight

Continental Waterways

Hot air balloon aficionados, wine enthusiasts, bicycling buffs and all those who enjoy the good life will find particular pleasure on a carefree Continental Waterways Hotel Barge cruise through the wine regions of France. The seven fantasy barges of this line carry from six to twenty-four passengers and have splendid ports of call. You can travel to Chablis to visit the luxurious gardens and palace of Marie Antoinette, Napoleon and Catherine de Medici; Loire and Sancerre, where you'll watch china decorated at a ceramic factory in Glen; Burgundy, with its historic architecture and lovely scenery and wildlife; Champagne, where you'll tour Renaissance mansions and medieval churches, castles and fortresses; Bordeaux to see the castle that could be the setting for Shakespeare's *Love's Labors Lost*; and Alsace Franche-Compte to explore towns caught in history, including the 18th century village of Schreckenburg.

For lovers of fine wines, this is the perfect way to visit France's most renowned vineyards and wineries. Whether your ship is moored in the heart of a charming town or

Continental Waterways

historic village, or is gently floating along rivers and canals past the picture postcard setting, you will see places rich in history, culture and cuisine.

Daytime excursions include visits to cathedrals, celebrated châteaux, museums and vineyards, plus bicycle trips and hot air balloon rides. Whatever the countryside has to offer, the guests of the Continental Waterways Hotel Barge cruises are sure to experience since the barge crew has a close rapport with the local people. The cruises even come equipped with bicycles for passengers' daytime exploring.

Greeted with a champagne welcome, guests recognize the emphasis on wine from the moment they arrive. Wine tastings are held on board and a wine producer shows passengers his vineyard and cellars.

A charming setting for such delicious French meals.

Cruise Ship Cookbook

Master Chef Guy Megret is responsible for all menus and food preparation aboard the barges, and he is well qualified. He was born into a family of pastry chefs and has been in the food business since the age of ten, serving in various restaurants throughout France, including Regine's. His recipes are for the advanced French cook or the gastronomic adventurer, and are printed with both the European and metric measurements that Monsieur Megret has indicated and approximate English conversions so that you can try them out in your own kitchen. As he puts it, "Bon courage et bon appétit!"

Sauce Chasseur Comme en Bourgogne
(A sauce to accompany game or lamb)

11 shallots or onions
4 cups 2 tablespoons red wine (1 liter)
2 bay leaves
1 carrot, sliced in rounds
5 garlic cloves, crushed
1 branch thyme
A few sticks parsley
10 whole peppercorns
3 scant tablespoons cooking oil (3 soupspoons)
2 scant tablespoons mustard (2 soupspoons)
1 scant tablespoon butter (1 soupspoon)
3 scant tablespoons flour (3 soupspoons)
Salt to taste

Continental Waterways

Finely chop 5 shallots. In pan, combine these with wine, bay leaves, carrot, garlic, thyme, parsley and peppercorns. Bring to a boil. Add oil and pour over meat. Marinate 24 hours. Drain meat into a bowl and roast it as desired. Reserve drained marinade. In saucepan, combine mustard, butter and flour, and bring to a boil. Stir. Add salt. Chop remaining shallots. Add them, stirring rapidly. Remove from heat before shallots are cooked. Strain sauce and add to meat. Serves 6.

Sauce Pour les Croûtons aux Morilles

- 8 to 12 ounces morels or dried mushrooms (240 to 360 grams)
- 1 tablespoon butter
- 6 shallots, finely chopped
- 1 scant tablespoon flour (1 soupspoon)
- Salt and pepper to taste
- 1½ tablespoons cognac (2 centiliters or 1 shot glass)
- 7 tablespoons water (10 centiliters)
- ¼ cup fresh cream
- 1 teaspoon nutmeg
- Croutons, butter and oil

In saucepan, put butter, shallots, and morels, and stir for 3 to 4 minutes until there is a slight crackling noise. Sprinkle with flour and stir. Add salt and pepper. Add cognac. Add water and cream. Bring to a boil, stirring constantly. Just before serving, grate nutmeg over sauce and adjust seasoning. In pan, fry croutons with a mixture of butter and oil. Make a bed of the croutons and pour the sauce over it. Serves 4.

Megret Sauce Vinaigrette
(A salad dressing)

3 scant tablespoons mustard (3 soupspoons)
1 scant tablespoon wine vinegar or lemon juice
   (1 soupspoon)
Salt and pepper to taste
1¾ cups tablespoons oil (walnut, groundnut,
   sunflower or olive) or cream (16 soupspoons)
1 tablespoon shallots, garlic, chives or tarragon,
   finely chopped

Combine all ingredients. Makes enough for 4 salads.

Mousse de Poisson

Serve this dish with a suitable sauce such as Nantua or Dieppoise.

1 pound 10 ounces fish without bones or skin
   (750 grams)
7 tablespoons butter (100 grams)
6 eggs
2 cups 1 tablespoon cream (½ liter)
3 teaspoons cognac (1 centiliter)
Salt and pepper to taste

Blend all ingredients in mixer. Butter a mold. Add fish mousse mixture. Place mold in a pan of water and bake for 40 minutes at 425°. Serves 6.

Megret de Canard au Miel

This dish is especially good with a celery purée.

6 breasts of duck, sliced into strips
¼ cup butter
1 scant tablespoon flour (1 soupspoon)
1 cup dry white wine
1 cup stock or water
1 scant tablespoon green peppercorns (1 soupspoon)
1 scant tablespoon pink peppercorns (1 soupspoon)
3 scant tablespoons honey (3 soupspoons)
Salt and pepper to taste

Sauté breasts of duck in butter. Do not overcook. Add flour and stir. Mix in white wine and stock or water. Deglaze pan, stirring in any meat that has stuck to it. Add peppercorns, honey, salt and pepper. Mix and boil for 1 minute. Serves 6.

Chapter Nine

Floating through Europe

You'll find gracious and elegant living afloat on board the nine luxury hotel barges of the Floating through Europe Lines. The barges offer the ideal way to leisurely float down the rivers and canals of Europe, docking by picture-perfect villas, medieval cities, opulent castles, châteaux, forests, farmlands and harbors.

The Juliana cruises past windmills and through historic Dutch canals.

Floating through Europe

The barges are small—the largest holds only twenty-four passengers, the smallest just eight—giving each cruise an intimacy that mammoth ocean liners cannot allow. On the tours, you can float through the Burgundy wine country of France, the canals of the South of France, and Alsace-Lorraine. You can take a Champagne Country cruise that originates in Paris and sail past castles, cathedrals and caves. Or sail down the River Avon through Shakespeare country to see Shakespeare's own home, medieval houses and the same path traveled by Lady Godiva. The barges can also take you on a Royal River Thames cruise, a River Neckar cruise through Germany, and a Tale of Two Countries cruise through Holland and Belgium.

You'll find fresh flowers in your cabin and chocolates placed by your bedside at night—just some of the small amenities and fastidious attentions that the Floating through Europe line provides its passengers.

Excellent wine flows freely, and an international team of master chefs prepares gourmet meals with the freshest produce of the open air markets and specialty shops along the route.

Some of the dishes that are served are relatively easy to prepare and others are a challenge, but all the recipes are so delicious that they're worth a try.

Tarte Belle Helene

3⅓ pieces semisweet dark chocolate (95 grams)
3 tablespoons butter, softened (90 grams)
3 eggs
6 tablespoons flour (45 grams)
⅔ cup sugar (150 grams)

For topping:

>   Additional semisweet chocolate
>   Milk
>   Butter

In double boiler, melt together chocolate and butter. In separate bowl, beat eggs and gradually add flour and sugar. Add melted chocolate and butter. Bake at 350° for about 20 minutes or until done. Meanwhile, make topping by melting additional chocolate with a little milk and butter in double boiler. Coat dessert with topping while it is still hot. Serves 6 to 8.

Avocado Mousse

>   6 avocados
>   ½ ounce gelatin (15 grams)
>   Juice of 2 lemons
>   Salt and pepper to taste
>   Nutmeg to taste
>   Paprika to taste
>   1 cup 2 tablespoons cream, whipped
>   (300 mls)

Melt gelatin in a little water and leave to cool slightly. Peel and pit avocados and purée their meat. Mix in lemon juice, salt, pepper, nutmeg and paprika. Pour in gelatin. Gently fold avocado mixture into whipped cream.

Floating through Europe

Terrine de Légumes à la Mousse d'Avocat
(Vegetable Pâté with Avocado Mousse)

For Vegetable Pâté:

    4¼ pounds fresh carrots
    1 pound string beans
    2 pounds turnips
    4¼ pounds spinach
    2½ cups heavy cream
    6 medium eggs
    1 pound 1 ounce butter, unsalted
    White pepper to taste
    Salt to taste
    Granulated sugar to taste

For Avocado Mousse:

    3 avocados
    2 lemons, juice only
    Salt and pepper to taste
    2½ cups heavy cream

To prepare carrots: Clean and cut into julienne strips. Sauté in butter for 5 minutes. Add 1¼ cups cream and reduce until cream evaporates. Let cool. When cool, add 3 unbeaten egg *yolks*, and salt, pepper and sugar to taste.

To prepare turnips: Clean and cut into julienne strips. Sauté in butter for 5 minutes. Add 1¼ cups cream and reduce until cream evaporates. Let cool. When cool, add 3 unbeaten egg *whites*, and salt and pepper to taste.

To prepare string beans: Cut lengthwise twice. Cook in salted, boiling water for 2 minutes. Let cool in ice water to retain green color.

To prepare spinach: Sauté spinach in butter until leaves are soft. Cool softened leaves in ice water. When leaves are ice cold, place in strainer to dry. Wrap spinach in paper towel and wring it out. Put leaves in bowl and cut into large pieces. Add 3 unbeaten egg *whites*, and salt and pepper to taste.

To prepare Vegetable Pâté: Butter a rectangular baking dish approximately 15 by 4 by 4 inches. Cover bottom of pan with half of spinach. Layer other vegetables in the following order: carrots, string beans, turnips. Use remainder of spinach for final layer. Cover baking dish with aluminum foil and put it into a larger baking dish filled with hot water. Bake for 1 hour at 350°. Refrigerate overnight.

To prepare Avocado Mousse: Peel avocados and cut into large pieces. Put in blender or food processor. Add full amount of heavy cream. Add lemon juice. Salt and pepper to taste. Blend mixture until thick enough to use in pastry tube. Remove Vegetable Pâté from baking dish. Slice and serve on individual plates. Using pastry tube, decorate each slice with mousse. Good when served with a green and red salad with a Lys dressing (instructions follow). Serves 15.

Lys Salad Dressing

⅓ cup white wine vinegar
⅔ cup salad oil
1 teaspoon Dijon mustard
Salt and pepper to taste

Blend ingredients and shake well. Pour over salad of red and green lettuce.

Floating through Europe

Guinea Hen with Margaux Wine

If guinea hens are unavailable, you may also make this recipe with chicken.

    2 guinea hens, 2 pounds each
    1 bottle Margaux wine (a dry, red Bordeaux wine. Need not be expensive.)
    5 small carrots, finely chopped
    5 small white onions, finely chopped
    1 teaspoon thyme
    3 bay leaves
    Oil
    Butter
    Flour
    5 cups chicken broth
    2 cups small pearl onions
    1¼ cups heavy cream
    7 ounces Crème de Cassis
    Parsley

One day before serving, cut each guinea hen into 4 pieces and marinate in Margaux wine, carrots, white onions, thyme and bay leaves. On day of serving, remove guinea hen from marinade and let excess marinade drip off. Save marinade. In large frying pan, brown hen in oil. Move hen pieces to another large skillet; then add butter. Sprinkle hen with flour and add marinade to skillet. Add 4¼ cups chicken broth and simmer for approximately 20 minutes. While fowl is cooking, boil pearl onions in small pot for approximately 10 minutes. Add onions to skillet. Remove skillet from heat and place hen pieces on plate. In skillet, slowly add heavy cream and Crème de Cassis to sauce. Put hen back in skillet and reheat for several minutes without allowing sauce to boil. Add remaining chicken broth if necessary. Serve guinea hen with sauce in tureen. Garnish with parsley. Serves 4.

Haricots Verts Sautes au Beurre
(Green Beans Sautéed in Butter)

1 pound tiny green beans, fresh
½ cup onions, chopped
3 tablespoons butter

Clean and blanch beans in salted boiling water for about 5 minutes. Rinse in cold water. Sauté chopped onions in butter. Add beans and season to taste. Stir while reheating and serve immediately. Serves 6.

Tomatoes Provençales

6 tomatoes
½ cup onions, chopped
1 clove garlic, finely chopped
Salt and pepper to taste
Butter

Cut each tomato in half. Top with onions, garlic, salt, pepper and dab of butter. Bake in preheated oven at 300° for 5 minutes. Serve immediately. Serves 6.

Tarte Tatin
(Upside–down Apple Tart "Tatin")

For dough:

    8 cups white flour
    2 cups butter
    1 cup sugar
    1 teaspoon vanilla
    ½ teaspoon salt
    3 tablespoons water

For filling:

    3 pounds Golden Delicious apples (Cortland or any hard meat apples may be substituted)
    1 cup sugar

To prepare dough: Mix together flour, butter, sugar and vanilla. Add salt and water. Roll very fine and thin.

To prepare filling: Butter a deep-dish pie pan. Sprinkle with ½ cup sugar. Cut apples into quarters and arrange in bottom of pan. Sprinkle with ½ cup sugar, filling in empty spaces between apples. Glaze over a high flame for about 5 minutes. Cover with rolled out dough and bake at 250° for 20 minutes. Remove pan from oven and glaze over high flame again for 5 minutes. Turn pie pan upside down onto serving dish.

Tuiles
(A French-Belgian traditional cookie)

½ cup unsalted butter
1 cup confectioner's sugar
6 egg whites (medium-sized eggs)
1¼ cups almonds, shelled and sliced (approximately 10 ounces)
Handful flour

Mix unbeaten egg whites with confectioner's sugar. Add melted butter slowly while stirring sugar and egg whites. Add almonds. Add flour. Beat into pastry dough. Put teaspoons of dough on cookie sheet. Flatten teaspoons until square or tile shaped. Bake 5 to 10 minutes at 350°. Makes 2 dozen.

Sand Cookies

1½ cups unsalted butter
¾ cup confectioner's sugar
1½ cups flour
3 drops vanilla
3 tablespoons sugar

Soften butter with fork. Add confectioner's sugar. While stirring butter and sugar, gradually add flour. Beat into pastry dough. Divide dough into 5 portions and roll each portion into a cigar shape. Combine vanilla and sugar. Roll portions in vanilla-sugar. Cover with wax paper. Refrigerate overnight. The next day, slice each roll of dough into ¼ inch pieces. Put slices of dough on cookie sheet. Bake for 10 minutes at 350°. Makes 2 dozen.

Gratin de Pamplemousse

4 pink grapefruits
½ pint cream
3 egg yolks
3 tablespoons confectioner's sugar
10 tablespoons syrup of grenadine
2 tablespoons sugar

Using zester, remove rind from grapefruits in fine strips. Do not remove any of the white membrane. Simmer strips in grenadine with sugar and a little water until crystallized. Chop rind into pieces. Divide grapefruit into segments and remove membrane from each section, retaining any juice in bowl. Arrange segments of grapefruit in flowershaped designs in 4 ovenproof dishes. In bowl, mix together cream, confectioner's sugar, egg yolks and grapefruit juice. Pour over grapefruit segments. Bake in hot oven for 10 minutes. Garnish with crystallized rinds and serve. Serves 4.

Gigot d'Agneau
(Leg of Baby Lamb)

3 pound leg of baby lamb
Cloves of garlic to taste
Salt and pepper to taste
Red wine to taste
Fresh thyme to taste

Cruise Ship Cookbook

To prepare meat: Preheat oven to 300°. Remove bone from leg of lamb, prick meat with garlic cloves, and salt and pepper. Roast meat for 20 to 30 minutes, basting often. Remove from oven and keep warm. Save juices.

To prepare sauce: Add red wine and thyme to meat juices and heat over a high flame, stirring for a few minutes until well blended. Slice meat, garnish with vegetables if you wish, and top with sauce.

Gateau de Crepes

Guests will be delighted with the combination of flavors in this delicious meal.

For crepes:

>   6 eggs
>   2 cups flour
>   Salt and pepper to taste
>   2 cups milk
>   6 tablespoons Grand Marnier
>   6 tablespoons oil

To prepare crepes: Beat eggs thoroughly. Sift in flour, salt and pepper. Beat well adding milk, Grand Marnier and oil. Lightly coat crepe pan or small skillet with grease and heat. Remove from heat. Coat bottom of skillet with a small quantity of batter. Do not turn crepe. When done, turn pan to slide off crepe. Makes 24. Set aside.

Floating through Europe

For Sauce Mornay:

    3 ounces butter
    3 ounces flour
    3 cups milk
    Salt and pepper to taste
    Pinch nutmeg
    ⅓ cup cream
    4 to 5 ounces Swiss cheese, grated

In saucepan, melt butter. Add flour and cook a minute without allowing to brown. Remove from heat. Boil milk and beat into flour-butter mixture. Add salt, pepper and nutmeg. Boil for 1 minute. Reduce to simmering and stir in cream and Swiss cheese. Film top of sauce with milk to prevent skin from forming. Set aside.

For spinach filling:

    1 ounce butter
    1 tablespoon spring onion, chopped
    12 ounces spinach, chopped
    ¼ teaspoon salt
    ½ cup Sauce Mornay

In saucepan, melt butter. Add spring onion and cook for a moment. Add spinach and salt and stir over moderately high heat for 2 to 3 minutes. Stir in ½ cup Sauce Mornay. Cover and simmer 8 to 10 minutes, stirring occasionally. Correct seasoning. Set aside.

For cheese and mushroom filling:

    8 ounces cream cheese
    Salt and pepper to taste
    ½ cup Sauce Mornay
    1 egg
    ¼ pound mushrooms, chopped
    1 tablespoon spring onion, chopped
    Butter and oil

In mixing bowl, mash cream cheese with salt and pepper. Beat in ½ cup Sauce Mornay and egg. Sauté mushrooms and spring onion in a little butter and oil. Stir in cheese mixture. Correct seasoning. Set aside.

To prepare gateau: Preheat oven to 350°. Butter 8 to 9 inch round baking dish, suitable for serving. Center crepe in bottom. Spread with layer of cheese and mushroom filling. Press crepe on top, and spread with layer of spinach filling. Continue to alternate layers of crepe and filling, ending with a crepe. Pour Sauce Mornay over top, and sprinkle with 2 tablespoons Swiss cheese. Dot with small pieces of butter. Bake for 20 to 30 minutes or until thoroughly heated and slightly browned.

Crème de Courgettes aux Queues de Langoustine, Beurre Blanc
(Cream of Zucchini Soup with Baby Lobster Tails)

This soup is also delicious with jumbo shrimp.

> 2 pounds baby lobster tails or jumbo shrimp, peeled and cooked in water seasoned with salt and pepper
> ¼ cup heavy cream
> 1 teaspoon buttermilk
> 3 pounds zucchini
> 1 pound unsalted butter
> 1½ medium onions, finely chopped
> 3 tablespoons white wine

To prepare *crème fraiche*: Begin well in advance. In jar, combine heavy cream with buttermilk. Cover tightly and shake. Let sit for 8 to 12 hours. The result will be a thickened cream.

To prepare zucchini: In saucepan, cut zucchini into large cubes and cover with water. Add 4 tablespoons butter and 1 chopped onion. Boil 15 minutes. Purée mixture in blender, and then strain.

To prepare Beurre Blanc: Simmer remaining onion in white wine. Add *crème fraiche* and continue to simmer. Add remaining butter and stir away from flame. Stir in strained zucchini mixture and keep warm.

Divide baby lobster tails or shrimp among 4 soup bowls. Cover with soup mixture. Serves 4.

Ris de Veau en Laitue

Serve this dish as an appetizer.

If you wish, you may prepare sweetbreads and sauce 24 hours in advance and refrigerate them. You may also freeze them.

> 1½ pounds calf sweetbreads
> Slice of lemon
> Salt and pepper to taste
> 2 tablespoons butter
> 2 carrots, diced coarsely
> 2 onions, diced coarsely
> 2 shallots, finely chopped
> 1 clove garlic, crushed
> 1 teaspoon tomato paste
> 1½ cups veal or chicken stock
> ½ cup white Burgundy
> ¼ cup port
> 6 lettuce leaves, blanched

To prepare sweetbreads: Soak sweetbreads for 2 or 3 hours in cold water, changing the water once or twice. Drain, rinse sweetbreads, and place in pan. Cover with cold water, slice of lemon and a little salt. Bring slowly to a boil, skimming occasionally, and simmer for 5 minutes. Drain, rinse sweetbreads, and peel them, removing ducts. Reserve trimmings. Press sweetbreads between 2 plates and place a 2 pound weight on top. Chill.

To season and braise sweetbreads: Preheat oven to 350°. In saucepan or shallow casserole, melt butter. Add carrots and onions and cook until golden brown. Add sweetbreads, shallots, garlic, tomato paste, stock, white Burgundy, salt, pepper and trimmings from sweetbreads. Bring to a boil. Cover and braise in oven for 35 to 45 minutes or until very tender.

To prepare sauce: Lift sweetbreads out of casserole and let cool slightly. Strain cooking liquid into pan, pressing the vegetables well to extract juice. Add port and boil until glossy and well flavored. Whisk in butter, piece by piece, until sauce is slightly thickened.

To finish: Cut sweetbreads into *escalopes*—diagonal slices about ½ inch thick. Refrigerate sweetbreads in sauce. Blanch lettuce leaves by pouring boiling water over them until they are well wilted. Cool immediately with cold water. Wrap each piece of sweetbread in a lettuce leaf and spoon sauce on top. Serves 6.

Gratin Dauphinois
(Creamed Potatoes au Gratin)

    1 cup heavy cream
    1 tablespoon buttermilk
    8 potatoes
    1 clove garlic
    Butter as needed
    Milk as needed
    Salt and pepper to taste
    Gruyere, grated, as needed

To prepare *crème fraiche*: Begin well in advance. In jar, combine heavy cream with buttermilk. Cover tightly and shake. Let sit for 8 to 12 hours. The result will be a thickened cream.

To prepare potatoes: Peel potatoes and cut in thin

slices. Mash garlic well. Butter baking dish and add garlic. Arrange potato slices on bottom of baking dish. Add *crème fraiche* and enough milk to cover potatoes. Then add salt and pepper and top with Gruyere. Bake in moderate oven of 300° for 30 to 45 minutes. Serve very hot. Serves 6 to 8.

Mousse au Roquefort

This first course is *very* rich!

2 cups heavy cream
2 tablespoons buttermilk
6 egg yolks
6 tablespoons table cream
⅓ ounce gelatin (10 grams)
13 ounces Roquefort (75 grams)
3 egg whites

To prepare *crème fraiche*: Begin well in advance. In jar, combine heavy cream with buttermilk. Cover tightly and shake. Let sit for 8 to 12 hours. The result will be a thickened cream.

To prepare mousse: Beat egg yolks and table cream until thick. Melt gelatin in a little hot water. Add to egg-table cream mixture. Purée Roquefort in blender. Add Roquefort to mixture; then add *crème fraiche*. Beat egg whites until stiff, and then fold them into mixture. Spoon mousse into ramekins with paper soufflé collars. Refrigerate for a few hours before serving.

Floating through Europe

Mousse au Chocolate au Whiskey

1 pound semisweet chocolate, chopped
2 tablespoons butter
½ cup water
1 cup confectioner's sugar
6 eggs, separated
2 to 4 tablespoons bourbon whiskey to taste

In double boiler, combine chocolate, butter and water. Heat until melted, stirring continually. Add half the confectioner's sugar and stir until melted. Remove from heat. Whisk in egg yolks, one by one, followed by whiskey. Refrigerate. Beat egg whites until they form soft peaks. Sprinkle in remaining confectioner's sugar and continue beating until stiff and glossy. Stir ¼ whites into cold chocolate mixture and then gently fold this mixture into remaining whites. Spoon chocolate mousse into champagne glasses or ramekins and chill for at least 2 hours before serving. Serves 8. Mousse can be made a day ahead and kept in refrigerator.

Chapter Ten

Holland American Line

Adventure, relaxation and romance have been the by-words of the Holland America Line, which has been sailing from Fort Lauderdale, San Francisco, the Mexican Riviera, Vancouver and Anchorage for the past 112 years. The service aboard all three of the mammoth luxury liners in the fleet is superb—as is the decor. The interior of the S.S. Rotterdam is decorated with mosaics, tapestries, sculptures and other collectibles. The other ships, the M.S. Nieuw Amsterdam and M.S. Noordam, are fashioned in an attractive, contemporary style.

With health spas, pools, tennis and shuffleboard courts, well-stocked libraries and Computer Learning Centers where you can learn the joys of personal computing, it's hard to find reason or desire to leave these lovely ships. But do, or you may miss out on a ride in a horse-drawn surrey in the Bahamas, a glass-bottomed boat tour of the beautiful sea life of Tahiti, or a trip to the Peruvian Alps to view Machu Picchu, the ancient fortress city of the Incas.

All three ships feature continental cuisine. Dutch foods

are a particular specialty. After a workout in the spectacular ocean spa, a jaunt on the walkathon, or a vigorous dance lesson, you might be ready for some hearty Dutch fare.

Passengers enjoy Dutch delicacies aboard Holland America Lines.

One recipe, "Hutspot," has historic beginnings. It dates from 1573 and is served on every Holland America cruise. This dish is traditionally eaten on October 3rd all over Holland to celebrate the conquest of the invading Spanish Army.

Hutspot
(Dutch Chuckroast)

3 pounds chuckroast
2 pounds carrots
2½ pounds onions
4 pounds potatoes
4 tablespoons butter
1 quart bouillon or beef broth
Salt and pepper to taste

Peel carrots, onions and potatoes, and cut into fairly large pieces. In large saucepan, heat butter. Add meat and quickly sear on all sides. Reduce heat and add beef broth. Simmer for 1 hour. Add salt and pepper. Add carrots and continue cooking for 20 minutes. Add potatoes and onions and cook for 30 more minutes. If needed, add a little water, but be careful not to add too much since most moisture should evaporate. Remove beef from pan and slice ¼ inch thick. Thoroughly mix and mash the remaining ingredients and season to taste. Mixture should be fairly stiff, not soupy. Place on serving dish and layer sliced meat on top. Serve very hot. A little drawn butter may be served on the side. Serves 8 to 10.

Ertwensoep
(Dutch Pea Soup)

This ethnic favorite is frequently requested by Holland America passengers. It is usually served as a main course in Holland.

- 2 cups split peas
- 1 cup whole peas
- Water
- 2 leeks, finely chopped
- 3 onions, finely chopped
- 3 stalks celery with leaves, finely chopped
- ½ pound smoke bacon, unsliced
- 1 large ham hock
- 1 whole smoked sausage ring
- Pepper, freshly ground

Soak both types of peas overnight in just enough water to cover them. The next day, drain peas and place in large pot with 2½ quarts water. Add all other ingredients except sausage. Bring to a boil. Turn heat down and let entire mixture simmer for 1½ hours, stirring often. If soup becomes too thick, thin by gradually adding small amounts of water. Add sausage and continue simmering for 15 more minutes. Pepper to taste. Remove bacon, ham and sausage. Slice meat and serve on pumpernickel bread as side dish. Serves 6 to 8 in large portions.

Chapter Eleven

Highland Steamboat Holidays

You can have a helluva Highland fling while escaping the pressures of the workaday world aboard the S.S. VIC 32, the Highland Steamboat Holidays puffer ship which chugs through the lochs and canals of Scotland. A luxury liner this is not. In fact, passengers are advised not to waste their time shopping at Harrod's or Bloomingdale's for their cruise wear.

The VIC 32 is a coal-fired steamboat that sometimes spews forth clouds of dark smoke, making the deck and decksters black with smut and grime. But never mind that. Don't let a little dirt stop you. This is the fun way to leisurely tour the Scottish countryside, quays and towns.

Pure air of the sea-lochs, magnificent Hebridean sunsets and fishing villages enveloped in heather are all part of the scenic Highland experience. Along the route, you can throw out a line at Loch Ness and try your luck at reeling in the legendary sea monster or explore castles centuries old —as well as modern distilleries. You can bird watch, hill climb or bike ride along the banks of the cruise route. Just jump ashore—you're close enough!

Highland Steamboat Holidays

On board, you can be a layabout, or pitch in and help the engineer shovel coal or try your hand at steering the wheel—a perfect excuse to reward yourself afterward with a belt of traditional malt whiskey found nowhere else in the world.

The VIC 32 chugs past the lovely Scottish countryside.

The passenger accommodations are roomy and comfortable and there is plenty of hot water. The meals are served in an especially convivial, family atmosphere. Both passengers and crew break bread together at a long table in the quaint and cozy dining saloon. There is a wood burning stove in the corner to ward off the chill of those misty Scottish evenings, and a traditional oil lamp sways gently overhead, keeping time as the steamboat glides along. With the hearty Scottish breakfast, the lavish buffet lunch, tea time snacks, and a full course dinner, you won't be hungry. Be prepared to let out your belt.

The food is always fresh and satisfying with a Scottish nuance in everything that's served. Fresh cockles come right off a deep-sea fishing boat and the pastries are homemade. A plus is that vegetarians can be accommodated for meals if they give advance notice.

Highland Pâté

8 ounces chicken livers
1 medium onion, chopped
1 clove garlic, crushed
6 tablespoons butter
Choice of herbs, preferably fresh
Salt and pepper to taste
1 tablespoon brandy

Mix onion and garlic in 1 ounce softened butter. Add chicken livers and sauté for 2 or 3 minutes with chopped herbs, salt and pepper. Cook again for about 1 minute. Cool. Blend to smooth consistency. Melt remaining butter. Stir into mixture along with brandy. Pack into mold. Chill. Turn out and serve with melba toast. Serves 8.

Crunchy Mushrooms

12 ounces mushrooms, fresh or canned
2 cloves garlic
2 tablespoons butter or as needed
1 tablespoon flour
½ pint milk

For topping:

2 tablespoons butter
2 ounces bread crumbs
3 ounces grated cheese

Chop mushrooms. Fry mushrooms and garlic in butter until dark. Add flour to absorb excess fat and make a roux for cream sauce. Cook for 1 minute. Add milk and stir. Bring to a boil, stirring continuously. Simmer for 2 minutes. Place into individual ramekins.

To prepare topping: Melt butter. Add bread crumbs and cheese. Spread over top of mushroom mixture. Broil for 5 minutes. Serves 8.

Mid-Argyll Mackerel

This traditional Scottish main course is particularly good served with potatoes in their jackets.

> 4 whole mackerel
> Salt and pepper to taste
> 2 medium delicious apples
> 1 small onion
> 7 ounces cheddar cheese
> ¼ cup butter
> 2 to 3 ounces white bread crumbs
> 3 to 4 tablespoons dry apple cider
> Lemon wedges
> Parsley, freshly chopped

Preheat oven to 350°. Cut off mackerel heads and slit fish down belly. Gut mackerel and clean thoroughly. Dry with towel and season with salt and pepper. Peel and coarsely grate apples, onion and 3 ounces cheese. Melt butter over low heat. In separate bowl, mix apple, onion, cheese and bread crumbs together and bind with 1 tablespoon melted butter. Stuff mackerel with this mixture and secure opening of each with 2 or 3 wooden skewers. Skewers are not entirely necessary, but they help to keep fish neat. Grate remaining cheese finely. Place mackerel side by side in ovenproof dish and sprinkle 1 tablespoon grated cheese on each. Pour over fish remaining melted butter and sufficient cider to cover base of dish. Place in center of oven. Bake 25 to 35 minutes or until mackerel are cooked through and golden brown. Garnish with lemon and parsley and serve straight from dish. Serves 4.

Stuffed Pear Salad

    4 large ripe pears
    Lettuce
    6 ounces cream cheese
    3 ounces mayonnaise
    1 heaping tablespoon orange marmalade
    2 teaspoons Worcestershire sauce
    Salt and pepper to taste
    Tomatoes, sliced

Peel pears, cut in half, and remove cores with spoon. Place on bed of lettuce. Mix all remaining ingredients except tomatoes to a smooth paste. Pour over pears. Garnish with tomatoes. Serves 8.

Clinhes Ice with Hot Fudge Sauce

For Clinhes Ice:

    3 ounces whole-wheat bread crumbs
    ½ cup confectioner's sugar
    6 egg whites
    ½ cup 1 tablespoon sugar
    1 cup heavy cream, lightly whipped

For fudge sauce:

    ½ cup butter
    ½ cup 1 tablespoon dark brown sugar
    ½ pint whipping cream

To prepare Clinhes Ice: Mix bread crumbs and confectioner's sugar in ovenproof dish. Brown until crisp under hot broiler. Leave to cool. Whisk egg whites until stiff. Add sugar. Fold in cream. Add bread crumb mixture. Turn into 2 pint container and freeze until solid. Put into refrigerator ½ hour before serving to soften slightly.

To prepare fudge sauce: Place all ingredients in a double boiler. Melt slowly and bring to a boil. Simmer for 3 to 5 minutes. Pour over Clinhes Ice. Serves 8.

Atholl Parose
(A traditional dessert)

4 tablespoons oatmeal
2 tablespoons flaked almonds
4 eggs, separated
2 to 3 tablespoons whiskey
½ tablespoons confectioner's sugar
½ pint heavy whipping cream

Lightly toast oatmeal and almonds. Cool. Whip egg yolks, whiskey and sugar together until thick and creamy. Whip cream until stiff. Add oatmeal and almonds to cream. Fold cream mixture into yolk mixture. Whip egg whites until stiff. Fold whites into the creamy egg yolk mixture. Serve individually in ramekins or glasses. Serves 6 to 8.

Part Four
Recipes from Around the World

Chapter Twelve

Royal Cruise Line

Blending old world culture with the opulence of chic resorts, the Royal Cruise Line's Golden Odyssey and Royal Odyssey carry seafarers to virtually every port in the world. These ships travel to the very best of the sun-soaked southlands of Central and South America, Acapulco, Costa Rica and the Caribbean. However, if the Far East is more to your liking, they can take you there as well to relive the historic voyage of Marco Polo or travel to the Islands of South China and the Java Seas.

The popular Route of Marco Polo cruise is a 30 day around-the-world shipboard extravaganza. You'll travel through Greece, Israel, Egypt, Bombay, Sri Lanka and Singapore.

The primitive and the modern, the ancient and the timeless blend into one unforgettable whirl on the South China and Java Seas cruise to Singapore, Indonesia, the Philippines and Hong Kong.

The Odyssey ships also sail to Europe, Scandinavia and the Mediterranean, where you may retrace the paths of your forefathers.

Royal Cruise Line

Such a wide range of itineraries is reflected in the superb dining, with special dishes featured from great cuisines around the world. The international chefs on the Odysseys have chosen dishes from Greece, North Africa, Italy, the Riviera, the Mediterranean, the Caribbean and the Black Sea. It is possible for passengers to enjoy eight international meals in one day: early morning coffee and rolls at pool side, continental breakfast in the stateroom, full American breakfast in the restaurant, mid-morning bouillon, a deck buffet, luncheon in the restaurant, dinner, and a midnight buffet. And since chefs of the Royal Cruise Lines can adapt entrées to fit low salt, low cholesterol diets, everyone can indulge in the splendid food.

Washington Cream Soup

3 medium ears of corn
8 cups chicken stock
4 egg yolks
½ cup milk
½ cup heavy cream
Parsley, minced

Cook ears of corn in boiling water for 3 minutes. Cool corn and cut off kernels. Reserve. Heat chicken stock in medium-sized pot. In separate bowl, beat yolks, milk and cream. Slowly add mixture to hot soup. Now add corn and mix well. Serve hot in bowls. Garnish each serving with parsley. Serves 8.

Chilled Fruit Borscht with Red Wine
(A cold soup)

2 pounds mixed fruit (apple, melon), diced into ½ inch pieces
1 pound black grapes or ½ cup grape juice
½ bottle red wine
½ cup grenadine syrup

Peel and slice fruit and place in large bowl. Slice grapes in half and remove seeds. Pour in wine and grenadine. Blend well. Chill in refrigerator until very cold. Serves 10.

Cream of Celery Soup Lisette

1 large onion
2 medium potatoes
2 medium carrots
¼ cup peanut oil
1 tablespoon flour
8 cups beef stock
4 egg yolks
½ cup cream
½ cup heavy cream
1 whole celery heart
6 tablespoons butter

Peel onion, potatoes and carrots and slice into small pieces. Heat oil in large pot and add these vegetables. Stir for a few minutes and then add flour and stock. Bring to a boil and cook until vegetables are soft. Purée cooked vegetables and their liquid in blender or food processor. Put blended mixture into pot and let simmer. In separate bowl, beat eggs, milk and cream. Beat contents into liquid mixture. Cut celery heart into small cubes and boil for 2 minutes. Add heart to soup along with butter. Bring to a boil. Serves 6.

Christmas Consomme

   6 eggs
   2 cups whole milk
   Salt and pepper to taste
   4 gratings nutmeg, fresh
   6 cups consomme
   30 asparagus tips, boiled, fresh or frozen

Beat eggs, milk, salt, pepper and nutmeg together. Pour egg mixture into flat bowl. Put bowl in pan of hot water and place in low oven to bake. Do not allow water to boil. When egg mixture thickens, take it out and cut it into ½ inch cubes. Then begin heating consomme. Divide asparagus tips evenly among 6 soup bowls. Add 8 cubes of egg mixture and hot consomme to each bowl. Serve hot. Serves 6.

Youvarelakia with Lemon Egg Sauce

For Youvarelakia:

> 2 pounds ground beef, pork or veal
> 2 onions, grated
> 3 tablespoons dill, chopped
> 1 tablespoon mint, chopped
> 1 cup bread crumbs
> 3 eggs
> ¾ cup butter
> 1 cup rice, uncooked
> ½ cup water
> Salt and pepper to taste

For Lemon Egg Sauce:

> 2 eggs
> Juice of 2 lemons
> 2 tablespoons water
> 2 tablespoons butter, melted
> 1 cup broth from Youvarelakia

To prepare Youvarelakia: In mixing bowl, blend together meat, onions, dill, mint, bread crumbs, eggs and half of butter. Scald rice in the water for 5 minutes and add to mixture along with salt and pepper. Leave mixture in cool place for 30 minutes. Then shape mixture into round balls the size of small eggs. Arrange on bottom of large saucepan and barely cover with boiling water, pouring carefully so that meatballs do not break. Add remaining butter. Press each ball slightly. Cover and simmer for 30 to 45 minutes. Use some of broth to make Lemon Egg Sauce.

To prepare Lemon Egg Sauce: Beat eggs with lemon juice, water and butter until well mixed. Slowly add hot broth, stirring with wire whisk. Mix until thick. Pour over meatballs. Serves 6.

Veal "Kapama" Athenis Style

    2 pounds veal, cut into ½ inch cubes
    1 cup olive oil
    1 onion, grated
    3 cloves garlic, minced
    1 tablespoon flour
    ½ cup white wine
    1 pound ripe tomatoes, peeled, seeded and chopped
    ½ cup tomato paste
    2 cups water
    Salt and pepper to taste
    2 pounds string beans, fresh or frozen

In casserole, sauté veal in olive oil with onion and garlic, making sure that meat is brown all over. Add remaining ingredients, except green beans, and cook mixture for 30 minutes over low heat. Push meat to one side and add beans. Cover and cook for another 20 minutes over medium heat. Serves 6.

Cruise Ship Cookbook

Lucullus Veal Youretsi

2 pounds veal, cut into ½ inch cubes
Salt and pepper to taste
5 tablespoons butter
2 cloves garlic, chopped
2 pounds tomatoes, peeled, seeded and chopped
4 cups chicken stock
½ pound thin macaroni
½ pound feta cheese, cut into small pieces

Rub veal with salt and pepper. In roasting pan or casserole, place meat, 2 tablespoons of butter, garlic and tomatoes. Bake at 325° for 30 minutes. Add stock. Bring to a boil and add macaroni. Stir frequently to keep macaroni from sticking. If it appears too dry, add more stock. When macaroni is halfway cooked, add feta and remaining butter. Simmer 10 more minutes. Serves 8.

Veal Chef Moulas

2 pounds veal, cut into 1 inch pieces
4 cloves garlic
½ cup olive oil
Juice of ½ large lemon
1 teaspoon salt
½ teaspoon white pepper
1 teaspoon dried oregano
2 pounds potatoes, peeled and diced
1 pound tomatoes, peeled, seeded and chopped

In large bowl, marinate veal in garlic, oil, lemon juice, salt, pepper and oregano. Add potatoes and tomatoes. Mix well. Pour mixture into baking dish and bake at 350° for 1 hour. Serves 4 or more.

Psaria Plaki

½ cup olive oil
3 large onions, sliced
2 cloves garlic, minced
2 tablespoons butter
6 slices sea bass or similar fish steaks
2 teaspoons salt
1 teaspoon pepper, freshly ground
3 tomatoes, sliced
2 lemons, sliced
¼ cup dry white wine

Heat oil in large saucepan and cook onions and garlic until golden brown. In large baking dish, melt butter and arrange fish so that there is space between each slice. Sprinkle with salt and pepper. Put a tomato slice on each fish and top with a lemon slice. Spread remaining tomato and lemon slices around fish and add onions and garlic. Add wine and bake at 350° for 20 to 30 minutes. When serving, spoon sauce over each fish slice. Serves 6.

Beef Boerek with Avgolemono Sauce

For Beef Boerek:

    2 large onions, finely chopped
    2 tablespoons olive oil
    1½ pounds lean ground beef
    Salt and pepper to taste
    1 clove garlic, minced
    2 tablespoons parsley, minced
    ½ cup pine nuts
    6 tablespoons butter, melted
    2 eggs
    36 sheets filo pastry, 6 by 8 inches (available in specialty shops)

For Avgolemono Sauce:

    2 egg yolks
    Juice of 1 large lemon
    1 to 2 cups chicken, beef, veal or lamb stock

To prepare Beef Boerek: In 1 tablespoon olive oil, sauté onions until soft. Place in mixing bowl. In remaining oil, sauté beef, crumbling it with fork. Drain. Add beef to onions. Add salt, pepper, garlic and parsley. Sauté pine nuts in 1 tablespoon butter until golden brown and add to mixture. Add eggs. Combine all of these ingredients until well mixed. Take 1 filo sheet and cover remaining sheets with damp cloth. Brush filo sheet with melted butter. Top with second sheet and brush with butter. Divide meat mixture into 18 portions. Place 1 portion of meat filling on the 2 filo sheets. Fold the sides up about 1 inch. Roll filo up. Place seam side down on lightly greased baking dish. Repeat for remaining filo and filling. Bake rolls at 400° for 15 minutes. Makes 18 rolls, 3 per person. Top with Avgolemono Sauce.

To prepare Avgolemono Sauce: In mixing bowl, whisk egg yolks 2 minutes. Continue to beat egg yolks while gradually adding lemon juice. Then begin adding hot stock by drops. Continue until sauce is thick enough to coat back of wooden spoon. Yields about 1 cup.

Almond Puff Pastry

    1 cup water
    ¼ pound butter
    1 cup sugar
    1 teaspoon almond extract
    2 cups flour, sifted
    ¼ cup almonds, blanched

Preheat oven to 325°. In saucepan, combine water, butter, sugar and almond extract. Bring to a boil, and then simmer gently until butter and sugar are thoroughly melted. Add flour all at once. Beat vigorously. Cook over low heat for 5 minutes, beating constantly. Spread pastry in greased 10 by 15 inch jelly roll pan or 2 square 8 inch pans. Cut in diamonds with sharp knife. Put almond in center of each piece. Bake 15 minutes, and then run under broiler for 1 minute. Makes 1 dozen.

Spetziota

1 pound filets of red snapper, pompano, turbot or sea bass
½ teaspoon salt
Juice of 1 large lemon
2 cloves garlic, minced
2 tablespoons parsley, minced
2 tomatoes, seeded and finely chopped
½ cup olive oil

Spread filets skin side down on baking pan. Sprinkle with salt and lemon juice and let marinate for 30 minutes. Then preheat oven to 450°. Combine remaining ingredients and spread them evenly over fish. Lower oven temperature to 350° and bake fish 20 to 25 minutes or until it flakes easily with fork. Serves 4.

Sea Bass Spetses Island Style

3 pounds sea bass or whitefish
2 pounds tomatoes, finely chopped
½ cup parsley, minced
4 cloves garlic, chopped
1 cup olive oil
2 tablespoons lemon juice
1 cup white wine
Salt and pepper to taste

Wash and cut fish into 8 equal pieces. Put slices in well oiled baking dish and cover with remaining ingredients. Bake ½ hour at 250°. Serve slices separately and cover with sauce. Serves 8.

Cube of Pineapple, Crème de Menthe

1 large pineapple, peeled and cut into quarters
8 tablespoons crème de menthe

Pour 2 tablespoons crème de menthe over each pineapple quarter. Serves 4.

Walnut Pancakes

2 eggs plus 1 egg yolk
½ cup sugar
2 teaspoons lemon rind, grated
¾ cup walnuts, finely ground
3 tablespoons flour, sifted
3 tablespoons brandy
½ cup butter
¼ cup confectioner's sugar, sifted

In bowl, beat eggs and egg yolk. Add sugar gradually, beating until light. Add lemon rind, nuts and flour. Beat until well blended. Add brandy. Mix. Melt half the butter. Add to batter and mix gently. In 7 inch skillet, melt small piece of remaining butter. Pour 1 tablespoon batter into it. Turn pan back and forth to coat bottom. Make pancakes as thin as possible. Cook over low heat until golden brown on both sides. Remove from skillet. Roll up immediately. Repeat until all batter is used. Sprinkle with confectioner's sugar. Makes 36 medium-sized pancakes.

Chapter Thirteen

Society Expedition Cruises

Any exotic cruise adventure that you can dream of can become a reality on Society Expeditions cruises. The ships, the Society Explorer and the World Discover, travel to distant and colorful places, seldom seen by the average tourist.

From retracing sea routes of legendary explorers to landing where no one has been before, their cultural and wildlife expeditions are designed to provide new and exciting experiences. Leading experts—from archaeologists, historians and art historians to naturalists, ornithologists and marine biologists—are on hand to provide stimulating lectures and exceptional leadership on excursions.

You can book a cruise through the Chilean Fjords or the Lost Islands of the Pacific, including Bora Bora, Fiji, Easter Island and Pitcairn Island, where you'll meet descendants of the H.M.S. Bounty mutineers. Cross the Arctic Circle on the Northwest Passage cruise, watch birds, butterflies and monkeys along the mighty Amazon River, or cruise to Alaska and the Aleutian Islands. Sail the Orient through China, Korea and Japan or travel to the secret

Society Expeditions Cruises

islands of the Caribbean. Book passage on an Orinoco River Expedition to travel deep into the jungles of Venezuela. Cruise to Borneo, New Guinea and Indonesia, or explore Antarctica, where guides will lead you within feet of penguins. You can also visit the Galapagos Islands, where Charles Darwin, observing the wildlife found nowhere else in the world, formulated his theory of evolution.

The list of places to go, things to do is endless. The cruise ship guides delight in showing new passengers new places. Conservationists and preservationists, they design tours that will leave the land and wildlife unspoiled so that each new group of cruise ship visitors seems to walk on untouched soil.

All accommodations are deluxe, with every shipboard amenity, even if the destination is primitive. The food is topnotch, complemented by an extensive wine cellar.

For the gourmet, the Champagne and Caviar Cruise offers a unique experience. The World Discover takes you on an epicurean adventure through Nova Scotia to the secret islands of the Caribbean.

On this unusual cruise, passengers gather with foremost culinary experts to taste the world's finest foods. You can savor the subtle differences between the world's caviars, the nuances of the finest champagnes. An expert leads tastings of Burgundy's best wines. In addition, the chef and special guests will demonstrate just how to prepare an array of exotic and mouth watering foods. It is the ultimate in cruise ship dining from day one to day twelve.

Chef du Cuisine of the World Discover, Hans Baumhauer, shares his favorites:

Chilled Cream Soups

Cream of Coconut and Tangerine Soup

    8 ounces shredded coconut (about 3 cups)
    2 quarts vanilla ice cream
    2 cups half and half
    16 ounce can tangerines or mandarin oranges
    6 ounce can coconut milk
    Juice of 2 lemons
    Cognac to taste

Boil coconut in enough water to cover it. Let stand overnight. Soften ice cream and add all remaining ingredients. In blender, blend until smooth. Serve in chilled bowls. Garnish with more fruit if desired. Serves 6 to 8.

Cream of Orange Soup

    2 quarts vanilla ice cream
    1 cup frozen orange juice concentrate
    2 cups orange sections
    2 cups half and half
    Orange liqueur to taste
    Dash of rum
    A few drops of angostura bitters
    Grated orange rind from 2 oranges

Soften ice cream and add all other ingredients. In blender, blend until smooth. Serve in chilled bowls. Garnish with orange sections and mint leaves if desired. Serves 6 to 8.

Society Expeditions Cruises

Cream of Strawberry Soup

2 quarts vanilla ice cream
4 cups fresh or frozen strawberries
White wine to taste
Juice of 2 lemons

Soften ice cream. Place all ingredients in blender and blend until smooth. Serve in chilled bowls. Serves 6 to 8.

Veal Philippe

Chef Baumhauer says, "I had the idea for this combination on a South Seas cruise of 60 days duration. After 30 days, one has to come up with something different!"

8 veal scallops, cut ½ inch thick
3 tablespoons clarified butter
8 thin slices smoked salmon
16 slices avocado
2 cups Hollandaise sauce
¼ cup fresh dill, chopped, or 1 tablespoon dried dill weed

Slightly flatten scallops with flat edge of knife. Place butter in frying pan and heat. Lightly pan-fry veal, a few pieces at a time. Keep warm until all pieces are fried. Place one scallop on warmed serving dish and top with slice of smoked salmon and 2 slices avocado. Then heat Hollandaise sauce and stir in dill. Pour about 2 tablespoons sauce over veal, salmon and avocado. Serve at once. Serves 8.

Bami Goreng
(Indonesian Style Fried Noodles and Vegetables)

1 pound egg noodles
Peanut oil
2 medium onions, chopped
2 cloves garlic
1 medium cauliflower, cut into chunks
4 celery stalks, sliced
1 medium cabbage, sliced
½ pound bean sprouts
4 young leeks
½ inch ginger root, peeled and finely chopped
Sambal paste or 1 fresh red chili, seeded and sliced
1 tablespoon peanut butter
1 teaspoon ground coriander
½ teaspoon pepper
½ pound beef loin, thinly sliced
½ pound prawns, shelled
Thin slices lemon, cucumber and tomatoes
Thin strips omelet
Salt and pepper to taste

Cook egg noodles, rinse in cold water and drain well. Set aside. Coat bottom of skillet lightly with peanut oil. Add onions, garlic, cauliflower, celery, cabbage, bean sprouts, leeks and ginger. Fry until just crisp. Add sambal paste or chili, peanut butter, coriander and pepper, and mix well. Set aside. Coat bottom of another pan with oil and stir fry beef and then prawns. Mix together noodles, vegetables, meat and prawns, adding salt and pepper to taste. Pile on large, warmed platter and garnish with lemon, cucumber, tomatoes and omelet. Serves 8.

Part Five
American Dishes

Chapter Fourteen

American Hawaii Cruises

You'll find a perfect blend of elegance and relaxation on the Independence and Constitution, the American Hawaii cruise ships and the only luxury liners to cruise the Hawaiian islands. The Constitution and Independence will transport you through all the splendor of our fiftieth state —from the volcanoes of Kona to the black sands of Hilo, the lush jungle growth of Kauai, the waterfalls of Maui and the coconut groves of Oahu. In addition, they can take you to the carefree islands of Tahiti—Bora Bora, where tropical fish of brilliant color will swim right next to you; Huahine where you'll be greeted by lovely flowers and forests and friendly island natives; historic Raiatea and Tahaa, the original birthplace of the Polynesian peoples; and Moorea, an island of cliffs, rocks and forests more breathtaking than any man-made architecture.

These are the cruise ships of movie stars, presidents and royalty. *An Affair to Remember*, starring Cary Grant and Deborah Kerr, and segments of the *I Love Lucy* show were filmed on board. The Constitution has the distinction of being the only American vessel ever christened by royalty,

American Hawaii Cruises

Her Serene Highness Princess Grace of Monaco.

Flowered leis, exotic cocktails, swaying hula dancers, Hawaiian music are all part of the "Aloha Spirit" aboard the cruise. Instructors will teach you to play the ukulele or to hula. If you plan to travel with children, these are the cruises for you. Enjoy romantic evenings and afternoons alone without worrying; with special, supervised parties, dances, games and treasure hunts to attend, young children to teens will always be having as much fun as you do.

For dinner, Executive Chef John Bulawan prepares native Hawaiian dishes that are pure Pacific dining pleasure, so *mai i' ai* (come and dine) in authentic Hawaiian Island fashion. His very favorite follows:

American Hawaii Cruises takes pride in its delectable Hawaiian cuisine.

Butterfly Island Prawns

1 pound prawns
¼ cup butter
¼ cup vegetable oil
¼ teaspoon salt
¼ teaspoon white pepper
1 bay leaf, crumbled
1 clove garlic, crushed
½ teaspoon basil
1 teaspoon rosemary
½ teaspoon paprika
½ teaspoon dried red peppers
2 tablespoons barbecue sauce
2 tablespoons lemon juice
Parsley

You may serve prawns in shells or with shells removed. If you want to remove shells and clean, make this your first step. In saucepan, stir butter and oil over medium heat. Spread prawns out in pan, tails standing up. Sauté over medium heat. Add salt, pepper, bay leaf, garlic, basil, rosemary, paprika, red peppers and barbecue sauce, stirring continually. Pour lemon juice over cooked prawns before removing from pan. Garnish with parsley. Serve with rice and fresh vegetables. Serves 4.

Chapter Fifteen

Delta Queen Steamboat Company

Gracious dining on the river became a glorious tradition during the Great Steamboat Era of the early 1800's and it continues today aboard the legendary steamboat Delta Queen® and the magnificent Mississippi Queen®*, which cruise the Mississippi and Ohio Rivers. Sip a mint julep while you enjoy a Dixieland Band, or stroll the promenade on deck to the romantic sound of water cascading over the paddlewheel. You can easily fantasize that you are a Mississippi riverboat gambler or a hoop skirted Southern belle from a bygone era.

The Delta Queen Steamboat Company traces its roots to 1890 when the first paddlewheeler navigated the Ohio. It was at this time that certain steamboat sayings crept into the English language. The fluted smoke stacks on steamboats became synonymous with wealth and power. Hence, a large, powerful steamboat might be called "well stacked," a wealthy passenger, "high f-lutin'."

---

*Delta Queen and Mississippi Queen are registered service marks of the Delta Queen Steamboat Company, New Orleans, Louisiana.

Passengers appreciate delicious meals and excellent service aboard the Delta Queen.

Delta Queen Steamboat Company

Fried chicken, pecan pie, angel food cake and chocolate brownies were first served aboard steamboats, but Hotel Managers Robin Hixson of the Delta Queen® and Laird Segal of the Mississippi Queen®, prefer Creole cuisine on their river voyages today.

Omelet Creole

3 eggs
½ green pepper, finely chopped
Dash Tabasco sauce
Dash cayenne pepper
Pinch salt
½ teaspoon gumbo file
½ clove garlic, finely chopped
¼ onion, coarsely chopped
1 scallion, finely chopped
1 sprig fresh parsley
Olive oil
1 ripe tomato, peeled and finely chopped

Beat eggs until they are light and fluffy. While beating, add green pepper, Tabasco sauce, cayenne pepper, salt and gumbo file. In another bowl, mix garlic, onion, scallion and parsley. Combine with a few drops pure olive oil. Add tomato. Put half of these ingredients in batter and reserve half. Fry omelet as usual in omelet pan or frying pan. Top with reserved ingredients and serve.

Jambalaya

12 ounces chicken breast, chopped
2 smoked sausages, chopped
1 tablespoon oil
2 cloves garlic, peeled and chopped
1¼ cups white rice, uncooked
8 ounces tomato sauce
2¼ cups water
2 teaspoons salt
½ teaspoon cayenne pepper plus more to taste
3 bay leaves
10 drops Tabasco sauce plus more to taste

Brown chicken and sausage in oil. Add garlic. Sauté briefly. Reduce heat and add rice. Stir until rice is coated with oil. Add tomato sauce, water, salt, cayenne pepper, bay leaves and Tabasco sauce. Stir. Bring to a boil, and then simmer at lowest setting for 40 minutes or until rice is cooked. Serves 4.

Praline Sauce for Sundaes

¼ cup butter
2¼ cups brown sugar
4 ounces corn syrup
4 ounces chocolate sauce
½ pound pecans

Delta Queen Steamboat Company

Melt butter in saucepan; then add brown sugar and dissolve in butter. After sugar is dissolved, add corn syrup, chocolate sauce and pecans. Heat slowly, bringing mixture to a boil. Boil for 1 minute. Remove from heat and let cool. Will hold up forever—almost! Serve over ice cream or put in coffee. Makes 1 quart.

Flounder Olympic

This seafood fare is traditionally served at the captain's formal dinners.

    6 flounder filets of 6 to 8 ounces
    Butter, melted
    3 white onions, finely diced
    Salt and pepper to taste
    6 tablespoons mayonnaise
    2 tablespoons dill weed

Preheat oven to 400°. Butter sheet pan or casserole dish. Sprinkle with onions. Place filets on top of onions. Sprinkle with salt and pepper. With pastry bag or rubber spatula, spread mayonnaise on top of flounder. Sprinkle with dill weed and bake until golden brown, about 20 minutes. Serve immediately. Serves 6.

Shrimp Creole

1 pound large shrimp, cooked and peeled
1 white onion, finely diced
2 stalks celery, finely diced
½ bell pepper, finely diced
2 ounces butter
3 bay leaves
12 ounce can tomato sauce
10 drops Tabasco sauce, or to taste
1 teaspoon red pepper
1 teaspoon salt
1½ cups rice pilaf, cooked and hot

Sauté onions, celery and bell pepper in butter. When they become transparent, add bay leaves, tomato sauce, Tabasco, red pepper, shrimp and salt. Heat through for 10 minutes and serve over rice pilaf.

French Toast

French bread, at least 1 day old, sliced 1¼ inches thick
Eggs
Heavy cream
Pinch salt and pepper
Cinnamon and nutmeg to taste
Sugar

Delta Queen Steamboat Company

In bowl, briskly beat eggs and cream together. Add salt, pepper, cinnamon and nutmeg. Dip bread into mixture and soak through. Melt 2 inches of margarine in skillet and heat until just below boiling point. Add bread and brown on both sides. Drain toast and sprinkle with sugar.

Pepperdill Dressing

This recipe is the one most requested by Delta Queen® passengers. On the Delta Queen®, the dressing is served with a Steamboat Salad made from hearts of Boston lettuce and tomatoes.

    2 cups mayonnaise
    2 cups sour cream
    1 teaspoon pepper
    1 tablespoon Parmesan cheese
    1 tablespoon tarragon vinegar
    1 small white onion, diced
    6 drops worcestershire sauce
    1 tablespoon sugar
    2 drops Tabasco sauce
    1 tablespoon dill weed
    1 tablespoon dry mustard

Combine all ingredients and let sit for 1 hour. Serves 6.

Creole Pecan Pie

1 flaky pie crust
⅓ cup butter, chilled
½ cup brown sugar
3 eggs
¼ cup dark corn syrup
Dash vanilla extract
Pinch salt
2 cups pecans, finely chopped
Pecan halves, as needed

Cream butter and gradually add brown sugar. Add eggs one at a time and beat well by hand or an with electric mixer on *slow* speed. Add corn syrup, vanilla, salt and pecans. Stir well and pour into pie shell. Bake for 10 minutes in hot oven of 400°. Pie filling will then be set. Sprinkle pecan halves over top and continue baking for 30 minutes at 300°. Let cool and serve with generous helping of real whipped cream on top.

Southern Barbequed Spareribs

24 baby back pork ribs
4 cloves garlic, crushed
1 large onion, diced
Salt and black ground pepper to taste
1 bouquet fresh parsley, chopped
8 ounces tomato purée
2 teaspoons sugar
2 teaspoons tarragon vinegar

Delta Queen Steamboat Company

To prepare spareribs: Separate ribs with sharp boning knife. Wash and drain. Dredge spareribs through white flour. Sauté in skillet until brown. Remove from skillet and set aside.

To prepare barbeque sauce: Sauté in skillet garlic and onion. Sprinkle with salt and pepper. Add parsley and tomato purée. Mix well and keep simmering on low fire. Add sugar and tarragon vinegar. Stir well.

Add ribs to skillet and spoon sauce over them until they are well covered. Place in baking pan and bake in 300° oven for 45 minutes. Serves 4.

Crabmeat Stuffed Mushrooms

12 large mushrooms, fresh, stems removed and reserved
6 tablespoons butter
1 cup yellow onion, finely chopped
1 tablespoon flour
½ cup crabmeat
2 tablespoons fino sherry
1 tablespoon parsley, fresh, chopped
½ teaspoon salt
¼ teaspoon pepper
½ cup cornflakes crumbs

Preheat oven to 350°. Wash mushrooms and dry on paper towels. Place mushroom caps, top side down, on well greased baking pan. Finely chop mushroom stems. In 3 tablespoons butter, sauté onion until golden, about 5 minutes. Add mushroom stems and cook for 5 minutes. Stir in flour, crabmeat, sherry, parsley, salt and pepper. Sauté 2 to 3 minutes, stirring gently. Remove from heat and stuff mushroom caps with crabmeat mixture. Sprinkle with cornflakes crumbs and dot each cap with a pat of remaining butter. Bake 20 minutes and serve immediately. Makes 12 appetizers.

Oysters Vieux Carre

32 oysters
1 tablespoon onion, minced
Butter
3 tablespoon flour
2 cups milk, scalded
Salt and white pepper to taste
Sherry to taste
4 large mushrooms, chopped
2 shallots, chopped
Rock salt
Bread crumbs

Remove oysters from shells. Wash shells thoroughly and set aside. Wash oysters and chop coarsely. Sauté onion in butter until soft. Add flour and cook over low heat, stirring constantly. Remove pan from flame and add scalded milk, whisking vigorously until mixture is thick and smooth. Add salt, white pepper and sherry. Stir in mushrooms and shallots. Add oysters and mix well. Arrange oyster shells on a bed of rock salt. Stuff shells with the oyster ragoux. Sprinkle with bread crumbs and bake in 450° until hot and bread crumbs are golden brown.

Chapter Sixteen

Sea Breeze Florida Key Cruises

Calling all deep-sea fisherman! Does the Sea Breeze II have a recipe for you! This Florida Keys sailing vessel is a classic Chesapeake Bay boat, 40 feet long, spacious and comfortable. Sleeping only a cozy eight passengers, the Sea Breeze sets sail with its close-knit group for a day or a week, whatever it takes to insure you the most beautiful excursion through the coral reefs, sandy beaches and wildlife preserves of its itinerary. See exotic bird life or view a coral wall that rises fifteen feet off a sandy bottom. The captain, John Duke, is an old sea salt who is an expert navigator and tour guide, for he has sailed these waters many years.

The Sea Breeze II is a shallow draft boat and thus can sail in areas where other vessels cannot navigate—so an excursion on this boat is bound to be a unique adventure.

The standard meal makes a colorful table of various courses. Usually it consists of an entrée of fish or meat, vegetables, black beans, rice and a tossed salad. Captain Duke's ultra-specialty, however, is his fish chowder, and he says, "I do enjoy putting it together." Here is his favorite recipe, related in is own inimitable, sea-hearty manner:

Captain Duke's Delectable, Totally Irresistible Fish Chowder

1 fresh fish of any variety, whole
1 whole onion
3 fresh tomatoes, chopped or a 6 ounce can tomato
½ teaspoon basil
1 clove garlic
Salt and pepper to taste
2 handfuls fideos (pasta)

Spear, trap or buy a fish—snapper, grouper, jewelfish—whatever you like. Filet. Use head, wings and carcass for chowder. Waste nothing. Remove gills. Wash head and carcass well. According to number of people to be served, add water (2 quarts is about average) to nice sized pot along with fish remains. Boil for 15 minutes to soften meat in head, skeleton and wings. Then cool pot so you can handle it. Strain broth into second pot to eliminate scales and small bones. Pick remaining bones clean of all good meat. Put fish meat on small plate to await broth. Reheat broth on low flame. Add onion, tomatoes or tomato sauce, fish meat, basil, garlic, salt and pepper. About 5 minutes before soup is pulled off stove, add fideos to make noodle base. Use 2 handfuls—not enough to clutter pot but enough to enjoy with broth and fish. Continue to simmer on low heat until fideos are cooked. Pull off stove and it's ready to serve.

Sea Breeze Florida Keys Cruises

Delicious! Captain Duke says, "Of course the second day it's twice as delicious." Serves how many show up for dinner. Improvisations can be made to accommodate unexpected company. Should be good for at least eight to ten hungry people. Don't forget to give the cat some.

The Sea Breeze II.

Chapter Seventeen

Out O'Mystic Schooner Cruises

Would you trust a cruise line with a nineteen-year-old master chef who looks like a rock singer and never went to cooking school? You will if you are a true gourmet, a lover of exquisitely fine food or someone who simply appreciates the greatest cooking this side of a four star Paris restaurant. Richard Whelan, the chef extraordinaire of the Mystic Clipper, may be in his teens, yet he brings with him seven years of professional experience in the kitchen. He has fun in front of a stove and preparing meals for five to sixty-five passengers is his forte.

The Mystic Clipper, a 125 foot sailing ship, the fastest schooner on the eastern seaboard, combines maximum comfort with the exhilaration of adventure. Cruising the Chesapeake Bay and the waters of New England, the ship is a classic topsail, two-masted schooner. Her sister ship, the Mystic Whaler, is a replica of the sharpshooter schooners that cruised the world's whaling and fishing grounds at the close of the nineteenth century.

Cruises aboard either of the ships range from elegant evening dinner outings to five day sails. There are no organized social activities on board. Passengers can lounge about in total sybaritic indulgence, lazing in the sun, reading a good book or daydreaming to the roll of waves as the ship navigates the eastern waters. It's the perfect way to regroup, reflect and relax while having a high seas holiday that borders on the exotic.

Chef Whelan has explained how to concoct two special dishes, always favorites with his passengers:

Stuffed Flounder Whelan

12 flounder filets
½ pound lump crabmeat
½ cup white wine or vinegar
2 tablespoons tarragon
2 cups water
Juice of 1 lemon
1 teaspoon tarragon, additional
¼ cup mayonnaise
2 teaspoons Dijon mustard
1 teaspoon seafood seasoning
½ cup bread crumbs
½ teaspoon black pepper
1 egg

Mix wine or vinegar, 2 tablespoons tarragon and water. Marinate filets in this mixture for 2 hours. Then, mix together other ingredients. Line half the filets in baking pan greased with small amount of butter and a little water. Spoon 1½ tablespoons of mixture onto each of these filets. Cover each with a second filet and bake at 400° for about 15 minutes or until filets are flaky. Serves 6.

The Mystic Whaler.

Richard's Famous Stuffed Potatoes

6 baking potatoes
1 cup milk
½ cup instant mashed potatoes
1 cup water
1 tablespoon salt
2 teaspoons parsley
Pepper to taste

Bake potatoes at 400° for 1 to 1½ hours or until potato is soft when pierced with fork. Slice in half and scrape potato into bowl, reserving skins. Add other ingredients and mix until creamy. Pour mixture into pastry bag and squeeze into potato skins. Heat oven to 400° and bake for about 15 minutes or until tops are golden brown.

Chef Whelan at work.

Chapter Eighteen

Exploration Holidays and Cruises

You can cruise through the jungle rivers of Panama, sail to Bora Bora, Bali Hai and Tahiti, follow the Lewis and Clark route up the Snake River, party on the tropical waters of the Mexican Riviera or have a high Arctic adventure in the heart of Alaska—all on the aptly named Exploration Holidays and Cruises. Book passage on any one of the five ships in the Exploration fleet and you're off to one exotic port after another. The ships will transport you to small South Sea island villages, beautiful aquamarine lagoons, the seaports of charming Mexico, remote South American jungles and real Eskimo territory in the Arctic Circle. Since the ships are smaller than full-sized ocean liners, the captain can maneuver the vessel quite close to the breathtaking scenery and wildlife along the routes so that you can intimately experience the enchanting territory.

The atmosphere aboard ship is stylish yet informal and comfortable. Formal dress is never a requirement on the Exploration ships, even at the Captain's Gala Dinner. The casual attitude coupled with the intimacy that these small ships allow helps fellow passengers to become close friends in no time.

The itineraries are extraordinary and so is the food. Henry Wells, Managing Chef of the Exploration Holidays and Cruises, has selected his personal favorites:

Wilderness Chili

- 2 pounds ground beef
- 3 cloves garlic, minced
- 3 stalks celery, chopped
- 2 large onions, chopped
- 16 ounces tomatoes, chopped
- 8 ounces tomato sauce
- 1 teaspoon salt
- ½ teaspoon pepper
- 2 bay leaves
- 1 small can green chili peppers, diced
- 6 whole allspice
- 3 tablespoons sugar
- 15 ounce can kidney beans, drained and rinsed
- 4 tablespoons chili powder
- 4 teaspoons oregano
- ¼ teaspoon cumin

Brown meat. Drain. Add remaining ingredients. Cover and simmer for 2 hours. Serves 8.

Halibut Alyeska

3 pounds halibut steaks, boned
1½ cups sour cream
1½ cups mayonnaise
2 tablespoons onion, chopped
3 tablespoons lemon juice
Salt and pepper to taste
1 cup cheddar cheese, grated

Mix sour cream, mayonnaise, onion, lemon juice, salt and pepper. Spread over halibut. Sprinkle with cheese. Bake at 325° for 25 minutes. Serves 6.

Green Pepper Jelly

2 cups green peppers, chopped
5½ ounces jalapeno peppers
1½ cups vinegar
5½ cups sugar
10 drops green food coloring
½ bottle Certo

Place all ingredients except food coloring and Certo in large kettle. Boil for 5 minutes. Add food coloring and Certo. Stir well. Put in small, sterilized jars with paraffin. Makes 5 pints. Serve with cream cheese on crackers or biscuits.

Cruises aboard the Great Rivers Explorer are always an adventure.

Crab Salad Sandwiches

10 ounces crabmeat, fresh or canned
½ cup green pepper, minced
⅓ cup lemon juice
2 tablespoons onion, minced
¾ cup mayonnaise
Tabasco to taste
½ cup cheddar chesse, grated
6 English muffins, halved

In large mixing bowl, mix crabmeat, green pepper, lemon juice, onion, mayonnaise, Tabasco and cheese. Spread enough mixture on top of English muffins to cover. Bake at 350° until hot, approximately 10 minutes. Serve hot. Serves 6.

Curried Shrimp Sandwiches

1 pound baby shrimp
½ cup mayonnaise
½ pound cheddar cheese, grated
½ teaspoon curry powder
1 teaspoon worcestershire sauce
1 tablespoon lemon juice

In large mixing bowl, mix shrimp, mayonnaise, cheese, curry powder, worcestershire sauce and lemon juice. Spread enough mixture on top of English muffins to cover. Bake at 350° until hot, approximately 10 minutes. Serve hot. Serves 6.

Exploration Holidays and Cruises

Hot Bean Salad

2 large cans kidney beans
1 cup mayonnaise
½ cup celery, chopped
¼ cup cheddar cheese, cubed
2 tablespoons onion, finely chopped

Drain and wash kidney beans. Mix all ingredients together. Place in baking dish. Cover. Bake 20 minutes at 350°. Stir before serving. Serves 6.

Hot Chicken Salad

2 cups chicken, cooked and cubed
2 cups celery, thinly sliced
¾ cup mayonnaise
¼ cup mustard
2 tablespoons lemon juice
2 tablespoons onion, grated
½ teaspoon salt
½ cup cheese, grated
1 cup toasted almonds, sliced ¼ inch thick

Combine all ingredients except cheese and almonds. Spread on cookie sheet. Sprinkle with cheese and almonds. Bake at 350° for 15 minutes until bubbly. Serves 6.

Chutney Cheese Ball

8 ounces cream cheese, room temperature
½ cup prepared chutney
2 tablespoons curry powder
½ teaspoon dry mustard
1 cup pecans

Mix cream cheese and chutney. Add curry powder and dry mustard. Mix until creamy. Form into 2 or 3 balls and roll in pecans. Refrigerate.

Poisson Cru

2 fresh tuna, red snapper or halibut, skinned and fileted
½ cup salt
1 quart water
1 cup fresh lime juice
½ cup onions, coarsely chopped
2 cloves garlic, minced
2 medium tomatoes, coarsely chopped
1 medium cucumber, sliced
½ cup carrots, shredded
1 cup coconut milk
2 eggs, hard boiled and coarsely chopped

Slice fish thinly. Mix salt and water and soak fish for 45 minutes. Drain and rinse well with fresh water. Add lime juice, onion and garlic. Lime juice will "cook" fish. Let fish sit for ½ hour—longer if you want fish well done. Stir in remaining ingredients except eggs. Place on serving dish and garnish with eggs. Serves 6.

Poppy Seed Loaf

¾ cup butter or margarine
1 cup sugar
2 eggs
1 teaspoon orange peel, grated
2 cups flour
2½ teaspoons baking powder
⅔ teaspoon salt
¼ teaspoon nutmeg, ground
1 cup milk
⅛ cup poppy seed
1 cup walnuts, optional
1 cup raisins, optional

Beat together butter and sugar until smoothly blended. Add eggs, one at a time, beating well after each addition. Mix in orange peel. In a separate bowl, stir together flour, baking powder, salt and nutmeg until thoroughly blended. Add flour mixture alternately with milk to creamed mixture until well blended. Then stir in poppy seed, nuts and raisins. Grease and flour 9 by 5 inch loaf pan. Turn batter into it. Bake at 350° for 1 hour and 10 minutes or until bread begins to pull away from sides of pan and wooden skewer inserted in center comes out clean. Let cool in pan for 10 minutes; then turn out onto rack to cool completely. Makes 1 loaf.

Papaya Cake

- 3 cups flour
- 2 teaspoons baking soda
- 1 teaspoon cinnamon
- ½ teaspoon salt
- ½ teaspoon nutmeg, freshly ground
- ¼ teaspoon ginger
- 1 cup shortening
- 1½ cups sugar
- 2 eggs
- 2 tablespoons water
- 1 teaspoon lemon juice
- 2 cups papaya, diced
- 1 cup golden raisins
- Confectioner's sugar

Preheat oven to 350°. Grease and flour 2 quart brioche pan or 9 by 13 by 2 inch baking pan. In bowl, mix flour, baking soda, cinnamon, salt, nutmeg and ginger. Cream shortening with sugar in large bowl of electric mixer. Beat in eggs 1 at a time. Stir in flour mixture. Add water and lemon juice and blend well. Fold in papaya and raisins. Pour batter into prepared pan. Bake until tester inserted in center comes out clean, about 1¼ hours in brioche pan or 45 minutes in rectangular pan. Let cake cool in pan on wire rack. Turn cake out onto platter. Dust with confectioner's sugar before serving. Serves 12.

Peanut Butter Fingers

¼ cup shortening
½ cup sugar
½ cup brown sugar
1 egg
⅔ cup peanut butter
½ teaspoon baking soda
½ teaspoon salt
½ teaspoon vanilla
1 cup flour
1 cup oatmeal
½ cup confectioner's sugar
6 ounces chocolate chips
4 teaspoons heavy cream (plus a little more if necessary)

Mix together shortening, sugar, brown sugar, egg, ⅓ cup peanut butter, baking soda, salt, vanilla, flour and oatmeal. Spread in 9 by 13 inch pan. Bake at 350° for 20 minutes. Cover with chocolate chips and replace in oven for 1 to 2 minutes to let chips melt. Combine confectioner's sugar and ⅓ cup peanut butter with heavy cream. Layer over mixture in pan. Cut into thin "fingers" when cool. Makes 2 dozen.

Cruise Ship Cookbook

Bora Bora Brownies

These brownies are best when topped with whipped cream, ice cream or frosting.

- ¼ cup butter
- 4 ounces unsweetened chocolate
- 4 eggs, room temperature
- ¼ teaspoon salt
- 2 cups sugar
- 1 teaspoon vanilla
- 1 cup flour, sifted
- 1 cup pecans, chopped

Preheat oven to 350°. Melt butter and chocolate in double boiler. Allow to cool thoroughly or brownies will be heavy and dry. Beat until light in color and foamy in texture. Gradually add eggs and salt and continue beating until well creamed. Manually combine cooled chocolate mixture, sugar and vanilla. Before mixture becomes uniformly colored, fold in flour and pecans by hand. Bake in greased 9 by 13 inch pan for 25 minutes. Cut when cool. Makes 2 dozen.

Hello Dolly Bars

- 1 cup butter
- 1 cup graham cracker crumbs
- 1 cup walnuts, chopped
- 1 cup flaked coconut
- 1 cup chocolate chips
- 1 small can sweetened condensed milk

Preheat oven to 350°. Melt butter in 9 inch square pan. Sprinkle in crumbs and pad down lightly. Sprinkle on nuts, coconut and chocolate chips. Pour condensed milk over all. Bake for 25 minutes. Cook and cut into squares. Makes 2 dozen.

Pineapple Carrot Cake

3 eggs
¾ cup oil
¾ cup buttermilk
2 cups sugar
2 teaspoons vanilla
2 cups flour
2 teaspoons baking soda
2 teaspoons cinnamon
½ teaspoon salt
2 cups carrot, grated
½ cup crushed pineapple, well drained
1 cup walnuts, chopped
3½ ounces coconut (about 1½ cups)

Combine eggs, oil, buttermilk, sugar and vanilla, and mix well. Sift together flour, baking soda, cinnamon and salt. Add to mixture. Blend in remaining ingredients and pour into greased and floured 9 by 13 inch pan. Bake at 350° for 40 minutes. Cover with Buttermilk Frosting (following recipe) while cake is still hot.

Buttermilk Frosting

1 cup sugar
½ teaspoon baking soda
½ cup buttermilk
¼ cup butter
1 tablespoon corn syrup
1 teaspoon vanilla

Mix together sugar, baking soda, buttermilk, butter and corn syrup. Boil for 5 minutes. Remove from heat and add vanilla. Pour over carrot cake while cake and frosting are still hot.

Chapter Nineteen

Mid-Lakes Navigation Company

Scenic upstate New York is a blissfully peaceful setting for canalling—the way to go recreational cruising on a more intimate scale than the ocean liners. The Mid-Lakes Navigation Company, a Skaneateles based sailing company established in 1968, operates four vessels that transport passengers through the picturesque lakes, locks and canals of Rochester, Syracuse, Oswego, Buffalo and Albany. Seafarers can select any length cruise, from a dinner excursion to a one week sail through the historic wildernesses of the Mohawk valley.

The cruise line offers fall foliage tours, spring explorer excursions and summer escape theme cruises. You can glide past the beautiful mountain scenery and wildlife of the Finger Lakes, and take escorted side trips to pre- and post-Revolutionary War battle sites, through the deeply wooded mountains, and along the same route that early settlers traveled on their treks west.

Because the passenger capacity is small in comparison to transoceanic ships, the first class service on board all of the Mid-Lakes Navigation boats excels in individual attention and exceptionally fine care.

Navigating in the Mohawk Valley, where so much of America's history had its colorful beginnings, means traditional, simple, hearty American food—with a hint of international flavor thrown in as a tribute to the United States' ancestral heritage. The cruise staff is particularly proud of the New York State wine served on board, bottled under Mid-Lake Navigation's own label by one of the local vintners of the Finger Lakes region.

Apple Crisp

For Apple Crisp:

> 5 large apples
> ¼ cup brown sugar
> ½ cup white sugar
> ¼ teaspoon nutmeg
> 2 teaspoons cinnamon
> ½ teaspoon allspice

For topping:

> 2 cups flour
> ½ cup brown sugar
> 1 cup white sugar
> 2½ teaspoons cinnamon
> ½ cup softened butter

Mid-Lakes Navigation Company

Slice apples and combine with sugars and spices in bowl. Set aside. Combine all dry ingredients of topping. Cut in butter until consistency of meal. Put apples in lightly greased pan. Cover apples with topping. Bake at 350° for 35 minutes or until golden brown. Serve with heavy cream. Serves 6.

Passengers enjoy the beautiful mountain scenery of upstate New York.

Canaller's Irish Stew

1 pound boned leg of lamb, cut into 8 portions
½ pound Wideback bacon, cut into quarters
1 cup water
3 medium onions, 2 whole, 1 chopped
8 medium potatoes, peeled
1 teaspoon salt
½ teaspoon dry mustard
A good shake pepper
1 cup water

Warm saucepan and rub it with lamb fat. Add lamb, bacon and water. Slowly bring to a boil and simmer for an hour. Add onions, potatoes and seasonings. Cook until potatoes are done, about 30 minutes. Serves 8.

Spinach–Cauliflower Salad

1 small bunch spinach, torn into bite-sized pieces
½ medium head cauliflower, cut into small florets
½ cup pine nuts or slivered almonds
1 medium avocado
Lemon juice
1 teaspoon white pepper
½ teaspoon dry mustard
1 large clove garlic, minced or pressed
Dash ground nutmeg
6 tablespoons white wine vinegar
6 tablespoons olive oil
½ teaspoon salt
½ teaspoon basil

Mid-Lakes Navigation Company

Put nuts in baking dish. Bake at 350° until lightly browned. Set aside. Place spinach and cauliflower in bowl. Peel, pit and slice avocado. Dip avocado in lemon juice to coat. Add avocado and lemon juice to vegetables. In a separate bowl, combine pepper, mustard, garlic, nutmeg, vinegar, oil, salt and basil. Blend well. Pour over vegetables. Gently mix with nuts. Serves 6.

Canaller's Toddy

The chefs of the Mid-Lakes Navigation Company say that this grog recipe has been "tried and tested and is best enjoyed on the wet chill of an October evening."

- 1 teaspoon sugar
- 1 cup boiling water
- ½ slice lemon
- 3 whole cloves
- 1 stick cinnamon
- ¼ cup rum
- Nutmeg to taste

Dissolve sugar into boiling water in small mug. Add lemon, cloves, cinnamon and rum. Stir and sprinkle with nutmeg. Serves 1. Repeat as necessary!

Index

A

Almond Puff Pastry — 119
Appetizers—
  Avocado Mousse — 82
  Chutney Cheese Ball — 154
  Cocktail Meatballs — 26
  Coquille of Curried Seafood — 68-9
  Crabmeat Stuffed Mushrooms — 139-40
  Egg-Cheese Puffs — 29
  Fried Zucchini — 27
  Highland Pâté — 104
  Hummus-Bi-Tahina — 38-9
  Mousse au Roquefort — 96
  Ris de Veau en Laitue — 94-5
  Taramosalata — 28
  Terrine de Légumes à la Mousse d'Avocat — 83-4
  Tzatziki — 27
Apollo Pork Loin — 66-7
Apple Crisp — 162-3
Atholl Parose — 108
Avgolemono Chicken Soup — 21-2
Avocado Mousse — 83-4

B

Baked Stuffed Potatoes — 67
Baklava with Walnuts and Almonds — 32-3
Bami Goreng — 126
Beef—
  Bami Goreng — 126
  Boerek with Avgolemono Sauce — 118-9
  Bolognese Meat Sauce — 51
  Bourguigonne — 73
  Cocktail Meatballs — 26
  Hutspot — 100
  Moussaka with Eggplant — 30
  Ossobuco Milanese Style — 54
  Wilderness Chili — 149
  Youvarelakia with Lemon Egg Sauce — 114-5
Beef Boerek with Avgolemono Sauce — 118-9
Beef Bourguigonne — 73
Bolognese Meat Sauce — 51
Bora Bora Brownies — 158
Breads—
  Caribbean Dark Bread — 12
  Poppy Seed Loaf — 155
Bread Salad — 24
Butterfly Island Prawns — 130
Buttermilk Frosting — 160

C

Cakes and Pastries—
  Almond Puff Pastry — 119
  Apple Crisp — 162-3
  Baklava with Walnuts and Almonds — 32-3
  Buttermilk Frosting — 160
  Creole Pecan Pie — 138
  Dolce Monte Bianco — 54-5

Kunafah	36-7	Peanut Butter Fingers	157
Loukamades	22-3	Sand Cookies	88
Papaya Cake	156	Tuiles	88
Pineapple Carrot Cake	159	Cocktail Meatballs	26
Pineapple Torte	64	Cold Cucumber Soup	60-1
Tarte Belle Helene	81-2	Coquille of Curried	
Tarte Tatin	87	Seafood	68-9
Walnut and Almond Cake	34	Crabmeat Stuffed Mushrooms	139-40
Canaller's Irish Stew	164	Crab Salad Sandwiches	152
Canaller's Toddy	165	Creamed Potatoes au	
Capon or Roasting Chicken in the Style of Game	70	Gratin	95
		Cream of Celery Soup Lisette	112-3
Captain Duke's Delectable, Totally Irresistible Fish Chowder	142-3	Cream of Coconut and Tangerine Soup	124
Caribbean Dark Bread	12	Cream of Orange Soup	124
Carrots Veronique	72	Cream of Strawberry Soup	125
Caviar	28	Cream of Zucchini Soup with Baby Lobster Tails	93
Chestnut Pie	55-5		
Chicken alla Cacciatora	53	Crème de Courgettes aux Queues de Langoustine, Beurre Blanc	93
Chicken Calvados	17		
Chilled Fruit Borscht with Red Wine	112		
		Creole Pecan Pie	138
Chilled Strawberry Soup	61	Crepes—	60
Christmas Consomme	113	Gateau de Crepes	90-2
Chutney Cheese Ball	154	Lady Wonderful Caprice	55
Clinhes Ice with Hot Fudge Sauce	107	St. Michel	59
		Crepes Lady Wonderful Caprice	55
Cookies—			
Bora Bora Brownies	158	Crepes St. Michel	59
Gingersnap Cookies	13	Crunchy Mushrooms	104-5
Hello Dolly Bars	158-9	Cube of Pineapple, Crème	

Index

de Menthe	121
Cucumber Salad	27
Curried Shrimp Sandwiches	152

D

Daoud Pasha	39-40
Delight of Shrimp "Las Vegas"	49
Desserts (see also Cakes and Pastries and Cookies)—	
Atholl Parose	108
Clinhes Ice with Hot Fudge Sauce	107
Crepes Lady Wonderful Caprice	55
Cube of Pineapple, Crème de Menthe	121
Gratin de Pamplemousse	89
Mousse au Chocolate au Whiskey	97
Praline Sauce	134-5
Dolce Monte Bianco	54-55
Drinks—	
Canaller's Toddy	165
Frozen Imperial	44
Homeric Special	45
Oceanic Special	45
Peach Bellini	45
Pina Colada	46
Pineapple Tropical Night Dream	47
Portofino	46
Tricolor	47
Yellow Bird	46
Dutch Chuckroast	100
Dutch Pea Soup	101

E

Egg-Cheese Puffs	29
Eggplant—	
Imam	33
Moussaka with Eggplant	30
Salad	29
Eggplant Imam	33
Eggplant Salad	29
Ertwensoep	101

F

Filet of Sole Marguery	65
Fish (see also Shellfish)—	
Captain Duke's Delectable, Totally Irresistible Fish Chowder	142-3
Filet of Sole Marguery	65
Flounder Olympic	135
Halibut Alyeska	150
Insalata De Calamari	63
Mid-Argyll Mackerel	105-6
Mousse de Poisson	78
Paillard of Salmon with Sorrel Sauce	16
Poached Filet of Sole al Aguacate	62
Poisson Cru	154
Psaria Plaki	117

Sayyadeya	40-2
Sea Bass Spetses Island Style	120
Spetziota	120
Stuffed Flounder Whelan	145
Veal Philippe	125
Fish with Rice	40-2
Flounder Olympic	135
French Toast	135
Fried Zucchini	27
Frozen Imperial	44

G

Gateau de Crepes	90-2
Gebratener Kapaun auf Wildbret Art	70
Gigot d'Agneau	89-90
Gingersnap Cookies	13
Giovetsi	23
Gratin Dauphinois	95
Gratin de Pamplemousse	89
Green Beans Sautéed in Butter	86
Green Pepper Jelly	150
Guinea Hen with Margaux Wine	85-6

H

Halibut Alyeska	150
Haricots Verts Sautes au Beurre	86
Hello Dolly Bars	158-9
Highland Pâté	104
Homeric Special	45
Hot Bean Salad	153
Hot Chicken Salad	153
Hummus-Bi-Tahina	38-9
Hutspot	100

I

Indonesian Style Fried Noodles and Vegetables	126
Insalata De Calamari	63
Island Noodles Alfredo	14

J

Jambalaya	134

K

Kunafah	36-7

L

Lamb—	
Canaller's Irish Stew	164
Cocktail Meatballs	26
Daoud Pasha	39-40
Gigot d'Agneau	39-90
Giovetsi	23
Sauce Chausseur Comme in Bourgogne	76
Lasagne Verdi	48
Leg of Baby Lamb	89-90
Lobster Virgin Islands	50
Loukoumades	22-3
Lucullus Veal Youretsi	116
Lys Salad Dressing	84

Index

M

Meatballs and Pine Nuts Coated with Tomato Sauce	39-40
Megret de Canard au Miel	79
Megret Sauce Vinaigrette	78
Mid-Argyll Mackerel	105-6
Moussaka with Eggplant	30
Mousse au Chocolate au Whiskey	97
Mousse au Roquefort	96
Mousse de Poisson	78
Mushrooms—	
Crabmeat Stuffed Mushrooms	139-40
Crunchy Mushrooms	104-5
Sauce Pour les Croûtons aux Morilles	77

O

Oceanic Special	45
Omelet Creole	133
Ossobuco Milanese Style	54
Oysters Vieux Carre	140

P

Paillard of Salmon with Sorrel Sauce	16
Papaya Cake	156
Peach Bellini	45
Peanut Butter Fingers	157
Pepperdill Dressing	137
Pina Colada	46
Pineapple Carrot Cake	159
Pineapple Torte	64
Pineapple Tropical Night Dream	47
Poached Filet of Sole al Aguacate	62
Poisson Cru	154
Poppy Seed Loaf	155
Pork—	
Apollo Pork Loin	66-7
Bolognese Meat Sauce	51
Canaller's Irish Stew	164
Crepes St. Michel	59
Lasagne Verdi al Forno "Gastronomica"	48
Southern Barbequed Spareribs	138-9
Youvarelakia with Lemon Egg Sauce	114-5
Portofino	46
Potatoes—	
Baked Stuffed Potatoes	67
Gratin Dauphinois	95
Richard's Famous Stuffed Potatoes	147
Poultry—	
Avgolemono Chicken Soup	21-2
Chicken Cacciatora	53
Chicken Calvados	17
Gebratener Kapaun auf Wildbret Art	70

Guinea Hen with Margaux Wine	85-6
Highland Pâté	104
Hot Chicken Salad	153
Jambalaya	134
Megret de Canard au Miel	79
Scallopine di Tacchino	52-3
Praline Sauce for Sundaes	134-5
Psaria Plaki	117

R

Ris de Veau en Laitue	94-5
Richard's Famous Stuffed Potatoes	147
Roast Lamb with Pasta Giovetsi Style	23

S

Saltimbocca alla Romana	52
Salads and Salad Dressings—	
Eggplant Salad	29
Hot Bean Salad	153
Hot Chicken Salad	153
Island Noodles Alfredo	14
Lys Salad Dressing	84
Megret Sauce Vinaigrette	78
Pepperdill Dressing	137
Skordalia	24
Spinach-Cauliflower Salad	164
Stuffed Pear Salad	106
Tzatziki	27

Windjammer Caesar Salad	13-4
Sand Cookies	88
Sayyadeya	40-2
Sauce Chasseur Comme en Bourgogne	76
Sauce Pour les Croûtons aux Morilles	77
Sauces—	
Bolognese Meat Sauce	51
Chasseur Comme en Bourgogne	76
Pour les Croûtons aux Morilles	77
Praline Sauce for Sundaes	134-5
Scaloppine di Tacchino Reale	52-3
Sea Bass Spetses Island Style	120
Shellfish (see also Fish)—	
Bami Goreng	126
Butterfly Island Prawns	130
Crabmeat Stuffed Mushrooms	139-40
Crab Salad Sandwiches	152
Crème de Courgettes aux Queues de Langoustine, Beurre Blanc	93
Coquille of Curried Seafood	68-9
Curried Shrimp Sandwiches	152

Index

Delight of Shrimp "Las Vegas"	50	Beurre Blanc	93
Lobster Virgin Islands	50	Ertwensoep	101
Oysters Viex Carre	140	Sayyadeya	40-2
Shrimp à la Mikrolimano	31	Washington Cream Soup	111
Shrimp Creole	136	Wilderness Chili	149

Shredded Pastry with Nuts and Syrup 36-7
Shrimp Creole 136
Shrimp à la Mikrolimano 31
Skordalia 24
Soups—
  Avgolemono Chicken Soup 21-2
  Canaller's Irish Stew 164
  Captain Duke's Delectable, Totally Irresistible Fish Chowder 142-3
  Chilled Fruit Borscht with Red Wine 112
  Chilled Strawberry Soup 61
  Christmas Consomme 113
  Cold Cucumber Soup 60-1
  Cream of Celery Soup Lisette 112-3
  Cream of Coconut and Tangerine Soup 124
  Cream of Orange Soup 124
  Cream of Strawberry Soup 125
  Crème de Courgettes aux Queues de Langoustine,

Southern Barbequed Spareribs 138-9
Spetziota 120
Spinach-Cauliflower Salad 164
Squid Appetizer 63
Stuffed Flounder Whelan 145
Stuffed Pear Salad 106

T

Taramosalata 28
Tarte Belle Helene 81-2
Tarte Tatin 87
Terrine de Légumes à la Mousse d'Avocat 83-4
Tomatoes Provençales 86
Tricolor 47
Tuiles 88
Tzatziki 27

U

Upside-Down Apple Tart "Tatin" 87

V

Veal—
  Bolognese Meat Sauce 51
  Chef Moulas 116-7
  "Kapama" Athenis Style 115

Lucullus Veal Youretsi Philippe	116 125	Hummus-Bi-Tahina Lasagne Verdi al Forno	38-9
Ris de Veau en Laitue	94-5	"Gastronomica"	48
Saltimbocca all Romana	52	Moussaka with Eggplant	30
Scallops Valle d'Auge	71-2	Richard's Famous Stuffed	
Youvarelakia with		Potatoes	147
Lemon Egg Sauce	114-5	Spinach-Cauliflower	
Veal Chef Moulas	116-7	Salad	164
Veal "Kapama" Athenis Style	115	Terrine de Légumes à la	
Veal Philippe	125	Mousse d'Avocat	83-4
Veal Scallops Valle		Tomatoes Provençales	86
d'Auge	71-2	Tzatziki	27
Vegetable Pâté with		Washington Cream Soup	111
Avocado Mousse	83-4		
Vegetables—		**W**	
Avocado Mousse	82	Walnut and Almond Cake	34
Baked Stuffed Potatoes	67	Walnut Pancakes	121
Bami Goreng	126	Washington Cream Soup	111
Carrots Veronique	72	Wilderness Chili	149
Christmas Consomme	113	Windjammer Caesar	
Cold Cucumber Soup	60-1	Salad	13-4
Cream of Celery Soup			
Lisette	112-3	**Y**	
Crème de Courgettes aux		Yellow Bird	46
Queues de Langoustine,		Youvarelakia with Lemon	
Beurre Blanc	93	Egg Sauce	114-5
Eggplant Imam	33		
Eggplant Salad	29		
Fried Zucchini	27		
Gratin Dauphinois	95		
Haricots Verts Sautes au			
Beurre	86		
Hot Bean Salad	153		

National Press Order Form
7508 Wisconsin Avenue, Bethesda, MD 20814
1-800-NA-BOOKS

The following National Press books are available at bookstores or by using this order form. Please send me copies of the books marked below:

Title	Quantity	Price	Total
Cruise Ship Cook Bk		$6.95	
I Feel Awful Cookbk (Food remedies for common ailments		$5.95	
Under Streets of Nice by Ken Follett		$5.95	
Persistence of Memory Biography of Dali		$15.95	

Add $1.25 per book for shipping

Maryland residents add 5% sales tax

Total:

Enclose check or put your credit card number below:
Credit Card number: _____   Circle one:
                                       MC   Visa

SIGNATURE _____
Send to:
Name: _____

Address: _____